YOUR PREFERRED FUTURE.

ACHIEVED.

Ten Critical Questions
For Nonprofit Strategic Planning

John E. Bauer, PhD

Copyright © 2019 by John E. Bauer

All rights reserved. No part of this book may be reproduced in any form or by any electronic or mechanical means; including information storage and retrieval systems, without permission in writing from the publisher, except by a reviewer who may quote brief passages in a review.

KDP ISBN 9781091812253

"We consulted with John on the development of our most recent strategic plan. Our final product continues to guide our work successfully."

Tracey Sparrow, President of the Next Door Foundation

"John was articulate, energetic and adept at working with us to produce a strategy with a cohesive mission and vision statement, as well as positioning and action plans. Essentially, this process honed our board's focus and awareness so that our journey can continue with renewed energy and an optimistic outlook for the future."

Michele Grall, Rotary Club of Wauwatosa

"John is a seasoned executive, has a strategic orientation and understands the need to build the leadership capacities of senior leadership and boards. He is warm-hearted, intuitive and perceptive."

Rick Stiffney, Retired CEO of Mennonite Health Services

Contents

Preface — xi

Introduction — 1
Your Story in Ten Questions

Question One — 9
What are you doing?

Question Two — 17
How are you doing?

Question Three — 23
What will your environment look like in the future?

Question Four — 35
What does your environment look like today?

Question Five — 43
What is your preferred future?

Question Six — 57
Can you get there?

Question Seven — 65
How will you know if you get there?

Question Eight — 71
How will you deal with the unexpected?

Question Nine — 85
How will you support continuous learning, thinking and acting?

Question Ten — 91
How will you tell your story, to whom, and for what purpose?

Conclusion	99
A Final Word	105
Appendices	109
End Notes	127
References	133
About the Author	137

Preface

I've had experience facilitating strategic planning throughout most of my 40-plus years as an executive in both higher education and social service organizations. From those experiences, I gained insight regarding what worked and what didn't. Beginning in early 2016 I set out to develop an alternative approach to strategic planning on behalf of a large senior services agency. As I worked with their leadership, I reviewed the strategic planning literature and began to put together my thoughts on how nonprofit organizations might better plan their futures – what I came to term as their "preferred future."

In a series of blog articles, I proposed ten simple questions which framed the content of this approach. After testing this model and receiving feedback that clients have found it to be a valuable tool, I decided to share the process in book format. Expanding and refining my original blog articles, I have compiled them into chapters with references to resources for further reading. Through this book, it is my intent to stimulate thinking. It is not to provide a *magnum opus* on the subject.

There are a number of things I am *not* trying to accomplish with this book. I am not offering a workbook. You won't find worksheets, forms, tables, questionnaires, surveys, checklists or other tools to answer the ten questions. What *I am* offering is a model based on real experiences with nonprofit leaders who shared with me what they needed from the strategic planning process. Appreciating that one size or method doesn't fit everyone, *I am* sharing an approach which can be customized to organizational size and context.

I am not offering a textbook on how to do strategic planning. You won't find lengthy and exhaustive reference lists or bibliographies. There won't be extensive chapters explaining in depth each step of the process. You *will* find concise summaries of concepts and relevant examples from my own experience. A few references and end notes will open additional doors for further research.

This book isn't intended to function as a "do-it-yourself" guide to strategic planning. What I have laid out is a thought process and some practical steps you can take to create a story around your preferred future. The reader will have to judge whether they have the capacity to implement this model without outside guidance and support.

I would be remiss if I didn't acknowledge the outstanding contributions I received from my partner in business and life, my wife, Sarayu Meraki. Her attention to detail, along with her creative suggestions, have helped me to avoid regressing into an abstruse academician and have transformed my often-stilted prose into understandable English.

I am also grateful to the generous CEOs and boards of directors who willingly collaborated with me as we developed this model of strategic planning together.

Finally, I'd like to offer sincere thanks to Dr. Richard E. Herman who offered numerous helpful insights and suggestions to improve the readability of this book.

Introduction

Your Story in Ten Questions

A strategic plan can be thought of as a story. It acknowledges the past, describes current realities and portrays a realistic yet aspirational future. Therefore, a strategic plan provides a script for understanding your organization and defining its preferred future. Because your story is dynamic and will grow and change over time, stepping back to ask some simple questions helps establish shared meaning as you engage in the strategic planning process. The initial telling of the story through a strategic plan also creates a baseline of data from which the organization can evolve and encourages a space where your organization's preferred future can be understood, anticipated and ultimately achieved.

There is nothing extraordinary or exclusive about the questions we're about to explore. I created and compiled them to recommend options for clients as we navigated the strategic planning process. Although there are an abundance of tools, systems, methods and models for strategic planning,[1] I use the process on the following pages because it is simple yet comprehensive. If your planning process doesn't somehow ask and answer these foundational questions, the end result doesn't usually serve the organization well. Something will be missing.

Through experience, I've learned that these questions become the outline of your strategic narrative. The resulting story will help your leadership team understand what the team is striving to accomplish and has the potential to engage your stakeholders in a powerful and effective way. Most important, you will realize a shared vision of your preferred future with a strategic outline to achieve it.

Here are my simple (but critical) ten questions:

1. What are you doing?
2. How are you doing?
3. What will your environment look like in the future?
4. What does your environment look like right now?
5. Where would you prefer to be in the future?
6. Can you get there?
7. How will you know if you get there?
8. How will you address unexpected challenges and opportunities?
9. How will you support continuous learning, thinking and acting?
10. How will you tell your story, to whom and for what purpose?

The following chapters will examine each of these questions in more depth. You will find suggested approaches for answering them and resources to assist you along the way. My hope for you is that you will ultimately experience the success of the strategic planning process outlined in this book and uncover your organization's ability to achieve its preferred future.

YOUR PREFERRED FUTURE.

ACHIEVED.

Ten Critical Questions
For Nonprofit Strategic Planning

John E. Bauer, PhD

> "Achievement happens when we pursue and attain what we want.
>
> Success comes when we are in clear pursuit of why we want it."
>
> Simon Sinek

Question One

What are you doing?

This question carries with it the expectation that your organization has a clear purpose for existence and that this purpose has been articulated in some kind of a mission statement. The reason for beginning with this prerequisite is to make sure that you are absolutely clear about why you are in business and that everything you do is somehow driven by the understanding of who you are, what you are doing and why you are doing it. As you plan your preferred future, "What are you doing?" becomes the question that focuses you on your current reality and helps you acknowledge the past that got you there. It also challenges you to think about your ability to fulfill that mission in the future.

Examining the Mission Statement

I have been mildly surprised to hear nonprofit clients tell me, "We don't need to take more time to review the mission statement. Our board just went through that exercise, we've approved it and we're fine with our current statement. Let's just get on with writing a strategic plan." I certainly don't wish to invalidate previous efforts to evaluate your mission statement. However, the strategic planning process really does need to begin with a careful analysis of what the organization is doing, with whom, how and why.

I've observed that many organizations treat this exercise as a necessary but annoying task that boards periodically conduct. On the one hand, it may be viewed as an opportunity to contrive a grandiloquent slogan. On the other hand, it may be greeted with disdain as if it has no relevance to what the organization does. One college president told me, "We don't need a mission statement. Our mission statement is what we

Your Preferred Future. Achieved.

do every day." Action is necessary to fulfill your organization's mission, but to do that you need to have a focus and clear story about who, what and why you are doing it.

I believe that mission for a nonprofit organization can be thought of as profit margins are in the private sector. Having a clear and effective mission statement for a nonprofit is as important as knowing market demand at a for-profit company. "If mission accomplishment is as important as profit attainment, why do most nonprofits not spend equivalent time in mission creation and monitoring? In reality, nonprofits often bungle this process. As important as missions are, nonprofits frequently go off in ineffective directions by relying on mission statements that can be little more than slogans" (Pandolfi).[1] So how does your organization create this clear and effective statement? Let's dig deeper.

Strategic planning needs to begin with a consensus of understanding around what your organization strives to accomplish by fulfilling its mission. Failure to seriously address its mission and how it is stated not only undermines the strategic planning process but will also likely contribute to ambiguity of purpose in the minds of significant stakeholders. Without careful analysis of your mission, strategic planning will at best become an unprofitable academic exercise incapable of providing the focus and discipline needed to achieve your preferred future.

Following are a few mission-related questions to consider which highlight the importance of examining your mission statement.

1. Why was your organization founded?
2. Who started it and why?

Question One

3. Are you doing the same thing today that the founders did on day one?
4. Who are partners in your mission? Do you serve the same population?
5. What will this population look like in the future?
6. Who supports your mission?
7. How do they perceive your mission?
8. What impact is your mission having?
9. Can you demonstrate that you are fulfilling your mission?
10. Can you measure the impact it has on the target population?
11. What do you think your mission will look like in five or ten years?
12. Is your mission sustainable?

A carefully crafted mission statement forms the critical starting point for meaningful strategic planning, ideally in an effective, one sentence statement. It will form the foundation upon which you will build strategies that proactively prepare for the future.

Building a Solid Mission Statement

So, what is a mission statement and what are its attributes? Koenig[2] suggests that every good mission statement has three pivotal elements:

1. Our Cause: Who? What? Where?
2. Our Actions: What we do.
3. Our Impact: Changes for the better.

Here is an illustration that stresses the attributes of helpful and unhelpful mission statements (Fig. 1).

Your Preferred Future. Achieved.

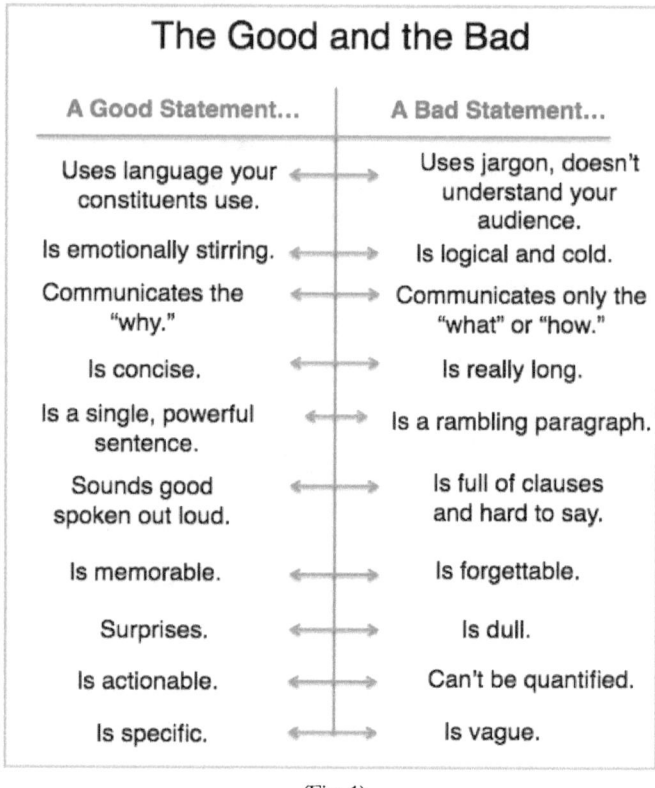

(Fig. 1)

The most effective mission statements are written in a single sentence of 15 words or fewer and contain all three of those elements. Here are a few examples to make the point.

- Public Broadcasting System: To create content that educates, informs and inspires.
- Environmental Defense Fund: To preserve the natural systems on which all life depends.
- CARE: To serve individuals and families in the poorest communities in the world.
- TED: Spreading ideas.

Question One

More than just serving as an inspirational slogan that employees and donors can get behind, Pandolfi[3] argues that "an effective mission statement must be a clear description of where an organization is headed in the future that distinctly sets it apart from other entities and makes a compelling case for the need it fills." In the same way that a clear and effective strategy in the private sector attracts more customers which results in more profit, a nonprofit's clear and effective mission strategy facilitates attraction of funds and provides the ability to take smart action while finding its own unique niche.

> What would the world look like if your mission was completely fulfilled?

If you think mission statements are old-fashioned, think about this: research at Ohio University shows that millennials especially are drawn to a strong mission. "Young employees want to believe their work is making a difference, whether they are in the for-profit or nonprofit sector. Good mission statements place the organization in the wider social context and show how the work of the organization contributes to making society a better place" (Fritz).[4]

An effective mission statement allows a nonprofit organization to operate with focus and discipline by providing consistency in decision-making. It also summarizes the means for measuring success and creates a shared understanding among all stakeholders that transcends time and place. In summary, an effective mission statement is translatable into measurable actions that everyone in the organization can understand, support, monitor and influence.

You might also ask the question: "What would the world look like if we fulfilled our mission?" Would hunger cease to exist?

Your Preferred Future. Achieved.

Would discrimination be eradicated? Would every child succeed in school? Contemplating "mission exits" like this can lead your organization to think deeply about how it measures its success. This can be articulated through a vision statement and can serve as a powerful expression of what you aspire to accomplish. A solid mission statement should suggest what that world would look like if the mission was completely fulfilled.

I believe that the process of creating a mission statement is as important as the end result. In the nonprofit world, boards of directors are the caretakers of the mission. CEOs are hired to advance and carry out the mission. Staff are directed to manage processes which support the mission. Donors provide financial support for the cause described by the mission. All these participants have a stake in the success of the organization, either morally (boards, donors and volunteers) or practically (paid staff). Engagement of all these stakeholder groups in the creation, review and analysis of the mission statement is one of the most effective ways to build support and loyalty.

I have sometimes found it challenging to help a leadership team understand that the process must begin with a thorough review of the organization's mission statement. However, if you take this vital step, you will inspire commitment and dedication toward developing a robust and effective strategic plan. Answering the "What are you doing?" question with openness and honesty builds the core elements around which your strategic narrative will evolve.

> "When you love people and have the desire to make a profound, positive impact upon the world, then will you have accomplished the meaning to live."

Sasha Azevedo

Question Two

How are you doing?

There is nothing wrong with envisioning and contemplating the future. But you have to be something of a realist in terms of understanding the world as it exists now, as well as how you contribute to improving that world by fulfilling your mission. In my experience, too many strategic planning efforts jump right into building a vision for the future without first carefully examining how well the current mission is being executed. This ignores present realities, both in the organization and in its environment, that may affect its ability to move toward its preferred future. Taking a long, hard look at how well you are carrying out your mission is vital as your leadership team and board chart a realistic path into the future.

Mission Impact and Sustainability

Traditional approaches to strategic planning often incorporate some form of SWOT analysis. However, I agree with Tom McLaughlin (pp. 101-102) that weaknesses and threats are really management issues better addressed through risk management processes, while strengths and opportunities are strategic issues requiring board and stakeholder engagement.[1] Furthermore, a SWOT analysis doesn't create space for reflection on the more significant, foundational questions that are relevant for nonprofit, mission-driven organizations.

> Mission fulfillment doesn't equal mission impact.

In the previous chapter I talked about the importance of having a strong, clear mission statement. But asking whether it's being *fulfilled* and measuring the *impact* of your mission aren't the same. If you were asked whether your organization

Your Preferred Future. Achieved.

is fulfilling its mission, you would probably say "yes!" This is what I would call a drive-by question. Fulfilling the mission? Yep. Check the box. Done and moving to the next attraction.

Ultimately, the question isn't, "Are you fulfilling your mission?" The question is, "What impact is your mission having on the people it's intended to support?" A SWOT analysis doesn't provide the high-level examination needed to explore that question. Other related questions might be, "How well are you executing your mission?" or, "Can you sustain your mission?". There are a variety of ways to quantitatively answer those questions. In any case, these are the types of questions that go beyond the typical review of the mission statement and which cannot be effectively answered by a SWOT analysis.

As an example of how you might conduct a study of mission impact and sustainability, Zimmerman and Bell provide a visual way to represent the perceived impact of your mission among the people you support against the profitability of each missional and fund-development program.[2] By mapping each program's net profit or loss against a measurement of mission impact, you can create a bubble chart. The size of each bubble is determined by the size of the expenditure budget. The relative position on the X-axis is determined by the amount of profit or loss (including actual, allocated, and shared costs) and the position on the Y-axis is determined by the overall score on the mission-impact survey. Following in Fig. 1 is an example which illustrates the value of this kind of analysis.

When your board sees the information represented in an example like this one, the "How are we doing?" question becomes obvious at a glance. However, it is still the follow up strategic questions that are of greatest value.

Question Two

- Can we be doing better?
- How do we move the bubbles to the right? Up?
- Which programs should we discontinue?

The end result is greater attention to mission impact and sustainability.

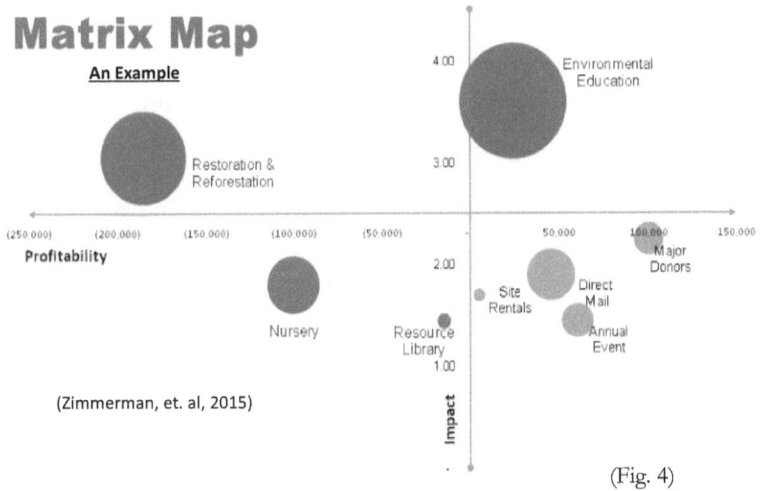

(Fig. 4)

I want to be very clear that an organization should not equate this kind of business model assessment with reviewing KPIs or other metrics of *efficiency*. For example, think about your car. Watching the fuel gauge, making sure the engine temperature is normal, logging regular oil checks – these are all valuable metrics, but only to a point. If the car is in neutral or up on blocks, it isn't truly doing what it was designed to do, and the performance metrics have become insignificant. The question that needs to be answered is "How well is the car getting its passengers to their desired destination?" If this car had a mission statement it might be, "To safely and comfortably transport passengers to their destination." Obviously, it is possible that the car could be running smoothly with all the gauges indicating optimal performance while failing miserably to achieve its purpose.

To translate this to your organization, efficient operation is not necessarily an indication that you are changing lives in the way that is implied or stated in your mission statement. Peter Drucker said, "Management is doing things right (efficiency); leadership is doing the right things (effectiveness)."

Therefore, having some type of business intelligence system is essential. The focus needs to be on promoting proactive thinking and acting, creating and using KPIs which monitor and guide future decision-making, as well as other metrics which support anticipatory leadership. Efficient operation is not necessarily an indication that the organization is changing lives in the way that is implied or stated in the organization's mission statement.

Quality

Getting closer to the heart of "How are you doing?" is the measurement of quality. Most nonprofit organizations track data around how their constituency groups perceive the quality of their services. These may come in the form of customer satisfaction surveys, third party assessments (often required by granting agencies), parent and guardian surveys, community needs assessments, etc. These tools may provide some meaningful insights into the impact your organization's programs are genuinely having on the people you support, but those tools more often identify measures of satisfaction and don't provide data related to the actual impact missional programs are having on people's lives.

Far from being a drive-by question, "How are you doing?" requires a deep analysis of the impact of the mission on the

Question Two

population and community being served. It requires deeper thinking around questions like these posed by Zimmerman and Bell: [3]

- If this agency didn't exist, who would it matter to and why?
- What is the social issue or human need the organization is trying to address?
- What does success look like and how would you know?
- Who are the primary direct beneficiaries of the organization?
- What is the geographic region of your impact?
- What is the scope of service?
- Are the missional programs delivered in an exceptional manner?
- How profound is the change affected in people's lives by the mission?
- How many people are impacted by the mission?
- Does the organization build community around its mission?
- Does the organization leverage relationships around its mission?

So, how well are you doing? Think about that question and the others posed in this chapter for a while before reading the next chapter. Taking the time to understand how much impact your organization currently has on the people it supports is essential. It not only will help you to address the next question on the list, but also will continue to expand the details of the story behind your strategic decision.

21

> "In strategy it is important to see distant things as if they were close and to take a distanced view of close things."
>
> Miyamoto Musashi

Question Three

What will your environment look like in the future?

Now that you have examined your organization's mission statement and conducted an honest appraisal of your current business model, it is time to focus forward. This step is necessary before projecting your preferred position into the future for two reasons. First, the current environment is guaranteed to change. Second, the future environment almost certainly will exhibit scenarios that you aren't equipped to manage right now.

Future First

You might wonder why I am suggesting that you predict the future before looking at your current environment? The main reason is that there is a natural tendency to project a future based only on the reality of your current environment. In essence, you are choosing a narrowed focus through a set of glasses, possibly ignoring potential future scenarios or limiting the types of questions you ask.

I'll use my bias against SWOT analysis to amplify this point. If you begin your planning with an analysis of the strengths, weaknesses, opportunities and threats as they currently exist, you are only looking at your organization like a snapshot in time. Even external factors like opportunities and threats are identified and evaluated in terms of the current status of the organization and its operating environment. Therefore, the tendency is to take each of those internal and external factors and evaluate what needs to be

> If I could predict the future, I wouldn't be writing about it!

done to either maximize strengths and opportunities or minimize weaknesses and threats. But the unanswered question is "To what end?" Merely addressing those factors for their own sake ignores the probable future in which the organization must function. If that future is going to demand a significant change in focus or mission, the analysis of current status alone is insufficient for describing the organization's preferred future and limits one's ability to think creatively.

Do the Research

Thinking about the future can be overwhelming, but it is essential to embrace the demanding research required to understand and respond to *future* social, cultural and demographic trends. This research should be focused on understanding the macro trends that will affect your organization, rather than your organization's current operating environment. This also has to happen in order to understand how potential future environments will affect your ability to fulfill your mission over time.

I have seen some nonprofits immediately move from the internal assessment discussed in the last chapter to a future mission based on a set of assumptions. This projection usually centers around things like the rate of inflation, turnover, cost of administration, market demand and a host of other environmental factors. Too often these assumptions are expressed in an incremental way, like "employee turnover will remain at 35% per year," or "the rate of inflation will hold steady at 3.5%." Consequently, organizations cast their vision by articulating strategies based on the false assumption that environmental factors will change slowly or even remain constant. In a strategic plan I was facilitating about ten years ago, I remember suggesting that an average annual return of 5% could be expected for the organization's endowment for

Question Three

the next 3-5 years. Then August of 2008 came along, the economy went into recession, the endowment lost 35% of its value and my assumption was shown to be ridiculously naive.

In reality, predicting the future is at best a carefully educated guess. If I could tell you with certainty what the world will look like in five years, I wouldn't be writing about it. But there are macro trends that can be recognized with comprehensive research. These trends need to be thoughtfully considered before putting a stake in the ground to claim your preferred future.

Following are a number of critical areas that warrant investigation. Searching out the best available research isn't necessarily easy, but knowledge specialists[1] within the organization as well individuals in the same service industry or academia who are conversant in the primary literature need to be sought out for trend data around relevant variables. Professional associations in human services are also possible sources of data collected on behalf of member organizations (e.g., AARP, Leading Age, AAIDD, HHS, VA, etc.).

Technology

As Alexa could probably tell you, no area changes as rapidly as technology. New and updated systems, apps and hardware are available every day. Innovative uses of technology to support people and deliver services are abundant. Technology-facilitated learning is changing the face of training, certification and stakeholder involvement. Business data has become business intelligence and is able to forecast and support proactive positioning based on statistical inference. Because of the rapid rate of change, it's challenging to anticipate how technology will support your mission. Advances in technology also have the potential to affect human resources, direct care, finance, marketing, funding and many others.

Population Changes and Demand for Services
Nonprofit organizations are, by definition, in the people business, so understanding the populations you serve and how those populations might change is essential. In the senior services sector, population distribution in various age cohorts can be analyzed, but it is asking an entirely different question when it comes to the types of services people will need or want. A question might be, "How do current models of independent living, assisted living, memory care, etc. align with growing preferences about aging in place?" In the world of intellectual and developmental disabilities (IDD), it's been shown that prenatal screening for birth defects and genetic anomalies contributes to higher rates of abortion. In this case, the question might be, "What is the rate of decline in the population of individuals with Down Syndrome or other disabilities who would benefit from our services?"

Studies of birth rates among ethnic and racial groups, reports on immigration and areas of settlement, descriptions of age cohorts in the future, longevity and life expectancy studies – all of these can be consulted to develop a best guess about the people your organization will support in the future.

Competitive Market
Most likely, there are other agencies in your geographic and/or service area that offer the same or similar services. It's certainly admirable that your organization came into existence and is still offering services to populations in need. But realistically, no one organization has exclusive rights to provide services in their sector. Businesses are

Question Three

going to continue to expand as long as there is a growing market or one that can be further penetrated. You may be the expert in your service area and support a loyal customer base, but if a larger provider decides to expand into your region, you're going to be challenged to compete.

> Competitors might be your best opportunities for collaboration.

Understanding the market and competition is critical for survival and positioning. You will have to discover or create ways to differentiate yourself and provide value.

Knowing who your competitors are and the relative shares of the market all of you serve is important for another reason. These competitors might be your best opportunities for collaboration. We currently see this happening in health care, but it is also increasingly common in social services, foundations and philanthropy. Merging multiple private school foundations can create pooled investment funds instead of competing for the same donors. On a mega-scale, think about Bill and Melinda Gates' Giving Pledge in which the planet's billionaires have been challenged to pledge their wealth to do good in the world. Knowing the competitive landscape in your future environment will help shape your thinking beyond your current environment.

Government Policy and Regulation

Closely monitoring government policies is of critical importance for organizations whose existence depends on the largesse of government. An analysis of the first two decades of the twenty-first century will illustrate the ebb and flow of government influence on how nonprofit organizations operate. While one administration multiplied

Your Preferred Future. Achieved.

the number of policies and regulations exponentially, a later administration made it a priority to roll back regulations. Some of the policy areas that can potentially affect nonprofit service organizations include environmental protection, health care coverage, taxes, immigration rules, entitlements, financial institutions and rules governing small businesses. Once some sense of the likely future is obtained, it can also help to advocate for the people your organization supports.

Revenues and Expenses
Most nonprofit organizations depend on a mix of revenues to support their operations. Public sources may include Medicare, Medicaid, Social Security, Supplemental Social Security, state and local assistance. Pensions and retirement and savings accounts are examples of private sources. The types of revenue a nonprofit receives depends on the population supported and the funding sources that are available. Individuals with intellectual and developmental disabilities depend almost exclusively on Medicaid, health care systems rely on grants and insurance carriers and private colleges and universities are supported mostly by tuition, donors and alumni.

Almost all nonprofits rely to some extent on donor support. Gift revenue can come from any number of sources including fundraising events, direct mail campaigns, major gift solicitation, planned giving, legacy and estate gifts. Many nonprofits also seek corporate and foundation support. Larger organizations may draw revenue from investment returns of endowments. Some have their own foundations. Unfortunately, the reality is that most nonprofits are too small and thinly staffed to capitalize on these non-operating revenue streams.

Question Three

There is also the area of social enterprise. If your organization provides supports to people who are able to produce a service or product that contributes to their own financial stability, there is mutual benefit. For decades, nonprofit service organizations have used vehicles like resale or thrift stores as a way to engage volunteers and the people they support to generate revenue. Others have incorporated green strategies to reduce utility bills and waste or applied micro-financing strategies to support client business start-ups.

Expenses also need to be examined, especially as you anticipate how costs will change over time, or if changes in your service model or delivery system will add or subtract costs to operations. Will technology offset some administrative overhead expense or make service delivery more efficient and cost effective? Will changes in government regulation potentially raise or lower expenses? Will health care reform lower the cost of employee health insurance? Is it more or less likely that labor unions will attempt to organize employees? Does leasing or owning vehicles/property make more sense? Should you explore opportunities to support international work or advocacy?

As we experienced in 2008, a downturn in the national and world economies can have a devastating effect on nonprofit revenues, making predictions about the future even more challenging. It is a generally accepted truism that funding of nonprofit social services is a leading indicator of market decline and a lagging indicator of market recovery. Cutting or delaying reimbursements for human services are among the first strategies states employ to balance budgets, while restoring or raising rates usually comes later. Knowing this makes it essential for leaders of nonprofit organizations to have trusted, informed and

Your Preferred Future. Achieved.

experienced counsel when making assumptions about the economic future. I was once given this half-joking advice: "Do your best to make assumptions about the future of the economy, but plan to be wrong."

Workforce Attributes

One of the biggest challenges facing most nonprofit organizations is hiring and retaining qualified, committed employees. Nonprofit wages are generally below those in the public sector. Entry level positions like direct support, food service, housekeeping, transportation and other unskilled jobs are plagued by high turnover rates due to low wages and/or the temporary nature of the jobs as employees finish school or pursue higher paying positions.

Who will your employees be in five years? Where will they come from? What is their age, educational attainment and aspirational attributes? How loyal are they to your organization? Do they work two or three jobs to make a living? What personal and family challenges do they face that can impact their reliability or longevity? What other qualities are they looking for in the work environment besides a salary and benefits? What are your attitudes about having employees work remotely? Is it possible to utilize flexible scheduling? How open is your organization to shifting its investment toward talent development rather than staff training? These and other questions will lead the organization to develop an employee profile for the future.

Location/Location/Location!

Where you provide services is the final critical planning element that warrants consideration for the future. If your organization is the only one of its type in a small town in northern South Dakota with the closest town of any size more than 50 miles away, this may not seem like much of

Question Three

an issue. However, if you are located in a suburb of the Chicago metropolitan area, location can play a significant role. Regardless, there are some questions to ask yourself as you contemplate where you will provide services in the future.

If your services are facility-based, are there opportunities to grow by building or purchasing remote campuses? Can you "franchise" your service delivery model to others by creating a collaborative service agreement where you provide the service if they provide the capital? If your services are community-based and are not as dependent on physical location, are there population areas that need your kind of service? For example, if you serve chemically dependent children and their families through in-home services, your geographic footprint is probably determined by how well you can manage your staff and the time it takes to drive to the client.

Finally, the geographical service area may be affected by collaborative efforts like a merger or acquisition. My work in developmental disabilities began when I helped facilitate the affiliation and eventual merger of two large service providers, one in the Midwest and the other on the West Coast. The resulting organization doubled the number of people we supported and turned a regional provider into a national organization. On a smaller scale, geographic expansion may occur through competitive bidding for services, like pursuing contracts to provide early childhood education. It may also happen by purchasing smaller for-profit agencies that help expand the geographic footprint of services.

Your Preferred Future. Achieved.

Looking forward suggests backward investigation in order to consider a preferred path for the future.

After reviewing all these future-focused questions and suggestions, it is important to come back to your mission statement. While it is essential to understand the probable future environment in which your organization will exist, you need to be prepared to consider the tension that may create with your mission. As you work to develop a framework for the future, begin to consider how your organization may need to change in order to fit into that framework. And even if your current mission is general enough or eternally relevant, the way you deliver it may shift, sometimes significantly.

Looking the future in the face can be frightening. There were times when I found myself gazing at the horizon out of my office window, contemplating the uncertainties of tomorrow and anticipating imminent challenges and opportunities. I couldn't help worrying about how the organization would respond and how well it would fit into the unknown. While we can't know with certainty what will happen, we can be curious observers. We can choose the team around us and become learners who are tuned into the world so we can make reasonable guesses about what the future will look like. Being open and willing to embrace or create what comes next is an essential step towards living out the goals of your organization's strategic story.

> Having the ability to be brutally honest with yourself is the greatest challenge you face when creating a business model.
>
> Too often we oversell ourselves on the quality of the idea, service, or product. We don't provide an honest assessment of how we fit in the market, why customers will buy from us and at what price.

Mark Cuban

Question Four

What does your environment look like today?

Question four is intended to identify areas of organizational strength that relate to essential planning elements as well as to call out gaps where the current status is not in alignment with the demands of the perceived future. It's different than question two, "How you are doing?" The answer to that question intends to measure the sustainability of your mission, the quality with which you execute your mission and the impact you have on the people you support. It is also different from question six, "How can you get there?". That question, though related, looks at the infrastructure, systems, policies, practices, leaders and the human and technological capital that support operations and make growth and improvement possible.

As I emphasized in a previous chapter, this does not mean doing a SWOT analysis. I strongly believe that examining your current strengths and opportunities are of strategic importance, while documenting weaknesses and threats invites your board to engage at a management level – something that is best avoided. Weaknesses and threats are more efficiently and effectively handled through a risk assessment and management process – not through strategic planning. Besides, when it comes to building your preferred future, as Tom McLaughlin asks, "Would you rather build it on strengths or weaknesses? We thought so!"[1]

Now that you and your team have explored the major trends that most likely will affect your organization's future, you're ready to turn attention to your current environment and analyze your organization as it operates today. You can use the

Your Preferred Future. Achieved.

same planning elements you worked through to predict the future, only this time you will evaluate your current position in each of those areas. Hopefully, the discipline of researching future trends and possibilities described in the previous chapter has accomplished two things: first, it will provide a framework to analyze your current status. Second, it will help move you to look outside any biases and promote more objectivity about your current environment.

If this is a bit confusing, allow me to describe a number of planning elements and demonstrate how future needs can be aligned with current realities. Let's take the same seven planning categories I suggested in the previous chapter. These recommendations are mine and aren't exclusive. However, I have observed that they broadly cover the most important dimensions of strategic planning and thinking.

> **Technology and Information Systems**
>
> How satisfied are you with the current IT system and associated infrastructure in your organization? Do you have a current plan and are you executing it? How is technology used to support each of your missional programs? Are some programs greater beneficiaries of technology assets than others? Are there significant differences among staff in your various service areas with respect to use? Do you have any power users? What are the strengths you have in IT that can position you to move forward? Is your current IT budget sufficient to meet organizational needs and keep pace with innovation? This is especially relevant to the systems needed to acquire, manage and manipulate data for business intelligence purposes.

Question Four

Population Changes and Demand for Services
What are the demographic attributes of the people you currently serve? What is the market niche in that population? Can you leverage your current position in the population to increase or expand the demand for your services? Are you adaptable in your current service lines to address the needs of new or different markets in the current environment? Is your organization the "gold standard" for the type of service you provide in your area? If not, then who is?

Competitive Market
Who is your current competition? Are they better, stronger or bigger than you? Is your organization the/a leading provider? Do your competitors take potential revenue away from you? Who are your collaborators? Who operates joint programs with you? Are there smaller, weaker or vulnerable organizations in your area that might be opportunities for collaboration or acquisition? What is your current market share and is expansion in that niche possible? Could you share administrative functions (HR, accounts receivable, accounts payable etc.) with competitors to reduce expense without affecting mission?

Government Policy and Regulatory Environment
How does government regulation affect your bottom line? Quality of services? Public perception? Are government agencies helpful to your work or do they present obstacles to efficient and effective operation? Do you have easy access to relevant government leaders and decision-makers? Do you participate in industry-wide advocacy efforts to advance awareness for your services and the people you support? Do you have sufficient leverage with legislators to advance your mission?

Your Preferred Future. Achieved.

Revenues and Expenses
What are primary funding sources for your operations? How strong is your advocacy position with government agencies to sustain financial support for your programs? What does your donor base look like and can its profile support sustainable growth? What percentage of operating expense goes to administrative functions? Do you have a process to proportionately adjust administrative costs when revenues fluctuate? If you had to cut 15% from your budget today, could you do so without diminishing the quality of your services? Do you have endowed funds or a reserve to cover unanticipated exigencies? Are programs funded by grants and if so, what is your success rate in winning them? How many days of operating capital do you have?

Work Force Attributes
How are your current employees positioned in order to maximize loyalty, professional growth, retention, promotion and commitment to the mission? What is your current turnover rate for all categories of employee? What are the skills required of current employees and how are those skills acquired, developed and improved? How are employees rewarded for excellent performance? How is employee performance evaluated? How are employees recruited, on-boarded, trained and retained? What is the age, gender, education, skill and experience profile of your current employees by job category? What does that profile need to look like in order to effectively operate programs and services at the appropriate level of quality?

Location/Geography
Where do you currently provide services and what constraints exist which limit your geographic reach? If you operate at multiple sites, how do you ensure coordination

Question Four

among units and their staff? What systems currently exist which promote smooth operation? Are there current opportunities to "franchise" your services in other geographic areas? Are there organizations with which you can collaborate to intentionally expand your service area?

These are only a few of the many questions that can be asked to describe your organization's current internal and external environment. Once answers are provided in the previous seven categories, you can begin to align the results with the work you did to predict your future environment. Comparing the current status of your organization with the projected environment it will face in the future will allow you to identify positions of strength as well as gaps which need more attention. These gaps are not necessarily weaknesses but could be areas of opportunity which can be developed to better position the organization as it continues to move into its preferred future.

> Weakness can be opportunities which can better position the organization.

Following (Fig. 1) is a simple diagram which describes the process I've laid out. Subjecting each of your major service lines to this scrutiny can allow you to obtain a clearer picture of the relationship between observable future trends and your current organizational reality. Bringing these into alignment provides the foundation for realistically describing your organization's future.

Your Preferred Future. Achieved.

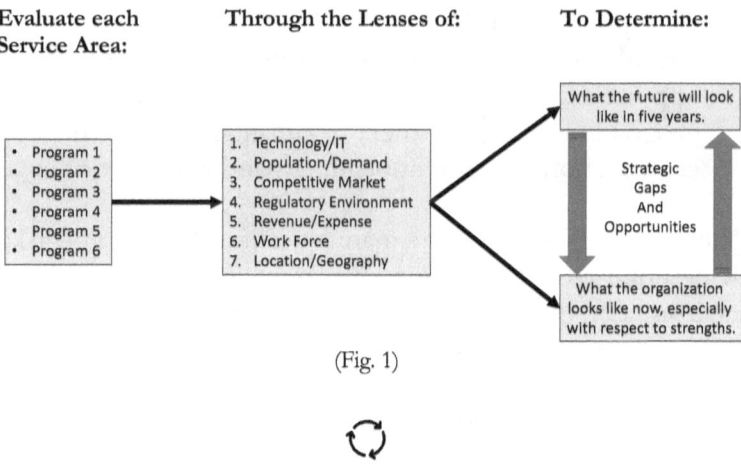

(Fig. 1)

I encourage you to take what is useful from this process and apply it to your own organization. You may have other key areas to identify or additional questions to add. Mapping the attributes of the future against your current organizational strengths will position you to answer question five with a greater measure of confidence and accuracy.

> "Excellence is never an accident.
>
> It is the result of high intention, sincere effort, intelligent direction, skillful execution and the vision to see obstacles as opportunities."
>
> Anonymous

Question Five

What is your preferred future?

Now that you've taken a look at your organization's likely future environment and honestly assessed your current operating position, you are ready to begin outlining the points of your strategic narrative (your story). Before suggesting how you can frame your future in words, I want to pause and reflect on an expression I use a lot in my practice, and frankly, what I believe is the only appropriate outcome of strategic planning: a living document in which your *preferred future* resides and is curated.

Why Your *Preferred* Future?

The truth is, there is always a set of ***possible*** futures, limited only by your vision and capacity to achieve them. If you analyze the world where you operate and are familiar with current challenges and changes likely to happen in the future, you might come up with a few ***plausible*** futures that are possible given your organization's recognized strengths and constraints. There is also a ***probable*** future if you continue to operate with minimal changes in mission or program. Understanding what that probable future looks like can serve as a baseline to help you measure risk or change. When choosing from a set of possible futures, leaders who are determined to position their organizations for maximum future impact and sustainability must describe the ***preferred*** future they are visualizing. The illustration (Fig. 1) following describes how these possible futures are related. I'd like to share a few observations on each of these so you can gain a better sense of

> Moving toward a preferred position will take some type of disruptive force.

Your Preferred Future. Achieved.

this thought process. There is also an inherent flaw in the model itself which I will expose and discuss at the conclusion of the chapter.

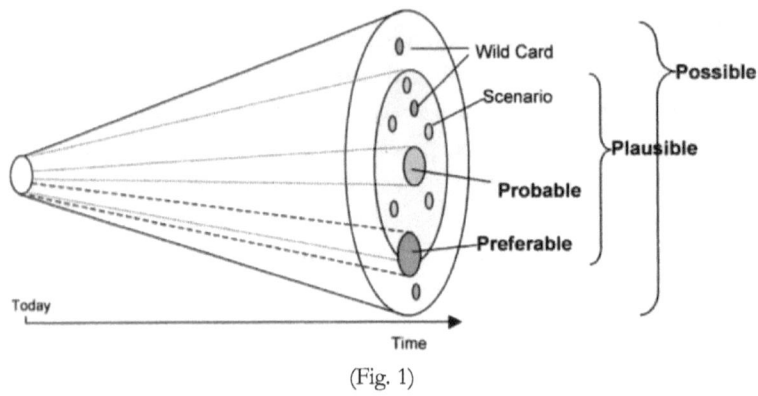

(Fig. 1)

Possible Future

So, what's possible? Well, just about anything! For example, if you receive an unexpected ten-million-dollar legacy gift, or the federal spending on Medicaid triples, you can dream big. It's possible that advances in technology will eliminate the need for direct care staff, that all your surrounding competition will turn their assets over to you, and that the state in which you operate will ask you to take over all state-run agencies of your type. Possible. But not likely. The key consideration is what is in your power to change. You can't predict when people will die and leave you multi-million-dollar legacy gifts. The political future is even less predictable. Fantasies, while tantalizing, need to fly on their own and not crash into the corn field of reality. As you attempt to describe various possible futures from a 30,000-foot view, you will come to realize that as you get closer to the ground with all its detail and variation, many of those possible futures are not realistic.

Question Five

Plausible Future
Okay. So, Uncle Fred isn't going to leave your organization the farm, the federal government will remain stable for the next five years, you'll still need a significant entry-level workforce and the competition will still wrestle with you for market share. Given the internal and external conditions in which you operate, what reasonable predictions can be made about the future and how will your organization fit into it? From the days when I taught logic, I emphasized the importance of an informal argument having both coherence and correspondence. Achieving plausibility is similar. A plausible future is one which must be internally coherent and consistent with current and projected realities. It also must correspond with how the majority of others in your industry view the future. A plausible vision of the future has to make sense, given everything else which is known. However, as Fig. 1 illustrates, the realm of the plausible is still pretty broad because of the large number of factors that could possibly affect the organization.

Probable Future
Probability is a mathematical concept which determines the likelihood of an occurrence. If you flip a coin in the air, the odds of it turning up heads is 50%. It is possible that you could flip it five times and get five heads in a row, but we know that the more instances of flipping a coin there are, the more probable it will be that 50% of the time you'll flip and get heads. In the world of organizational planning, we can also surmise the future based on daily, weekly, monthly and annual instances from the past, usually described quantitatively in terms of key performance indicators, benchmarks, financial performance, quality measures and whatever other ways exist to track your organization's behavior. Visually, you can graph

Your Preferred Future. Achieved.

performance which indicates behavior and change over time. Extrapolating those graphs into the future - including rate of change, arc and trajectory - you can determine a probable picture for the next 3-5 years. This assumes that existing internal and external conditions remain stable – a potentially dangerous assumption as I will discuss below.

Assuming you continue to do what you've always done with the same people in the same manner in the same location using the same methods, you can project a future based on past performance. If your strategy is maintenance, all you have to do is draw the lines five years into the future and clock out.

But that isn't why or where you want to lead your team, is it? It could be useful to think about what your organization would look like if you did nothing different, but merely creating a future based on current trend lines is a choice to fail the organization and ignore your responsibility to lead.

A real example will make this point. I was working with a church from a mainline protestant denomination that had been experiencing decades of gradual decline in membership, attendance, number of younger families with children, contributions and an increase in the average age.

> Creating a future based on current trend lines is a choice to fail the organization and ignore your responsibility to lead

In spite of a large, beautiful 130-year-old building, a new pastor, and a sizeable endowment, the church was experiencing a slow and painful death. Meetings with church leaders revealed a deep love for the

Question Five

church but an unwillingness to do things differently. I finally was able to capture their attention by asking, "Given the long-term rate of decline shown in the data, where do you think you will be ten years from now? Will it be a fine dining restaurant? A museum? An antique store? Because it won't to be a church!" The probable future was grimly obvious.

Wild Cards
Of course, the future is not perfectly predictable. As I previously mentioned, I was once the proud architect of a strategic plan that rigorously analyzed everything I've talked about here. This beautifully constructed vision for the future was enthusiastically adopted in February of 2008 by the board of the organization I was working for at the time. The following September it went into the ash heap of history as a useless stack of paper. The wild card we were dealt was called The Great Recession and it dramatically reshaped our future as we worked to survive. While many times unpredictable, possible wild card events need to be anticipated and risk mitigation strategies developed. The previous figure only indicates their possibility, not their probability. Acknowledge them but work to avoid them. Or, if you can't predict possible wild card events, make sure you have a process in place to rationally address them when they occur. A more detailed approach is included in Chapter Eight.

Preferred Future
Given everything you now know about what is possible, plausible and probable, what would you prefer your organization's future to look like? It should be noted in the diagram (Fig. 1) that the preferred future overlaps the possible and plausible cones of likelihood. What this implies is that moving the organization from the line of

probability into a preferred position is going to take some kind of disruptive force. Some significant change must take place to change the organization's path. Strategic thinking of this type must push people to consider alternatives and challenge conventional methods. "Bending the curve" of performance to reflect sustainable positive change requires insight into future possibilities and courage to lead in new directions.

Your preferred future should be written in the form of general, high-level strategic position statements. I prefer this terminology over words like "goals," "objectives," "strategies" or "initiatives", which have their own technical meanings and imply associated measurable targets and timelines. These types of statements will follow later as the leadership team develops annual action plans. For purposes of the strategic plan, boards need to focus solely on the high-level strategic positions and not be allowed to get into the weeds around tactical issues.

Defining Your Preferred Future

If you return to the seven planning variables laid out in the two previous chapters, you can define a preferred position in each of those areas. Collectively, they comprise the organization's vision for the future. Below are examples of what some high-level position statements might look like for each of the respective planning elements I've mentioned in Chapters Three and Four. If you'd like to explore what it looks like to develop these strategic positions, along with associated goals and initiatives, I have included two examples from actual strategic plans in the Appendices.

Question Five

Technology
In five years, the organization will be regionally recognized as the frontline innovator in the use of adaptive and educational technology to support people with intellectual and developmental disabilities.

Population/Demand
The organization will provide a comprehensive continuum of care to seniors beginning with early retirement and continuing to end of life with a dominant desire to meet their needs at every phase of life in their own homes.

Competitive Market
The organization will be the exemplar of excellence in its region and will strive to expand its mission of quality through affiliation, collaboration or merger with identified competitors in the region.

Regulatory Environment
The organization will aggressively advocate at every level of government to ensure the highest level of funding, client civil rights and legal protection for the people it supports.

Financial Position
The organization will ensure its long-term sustainability by building an endowment through aggressive fundraising from individual, corporate and foundation donors which will be of sufficient size to offset at least 50% of all corporate overhead expense from its earnings.

Work Force
The organization will be recognized in its region as the employer of choice, characterized by high employee satisfaction, lower than average turnover and opportunities

for all employees to grow and advance personally and professionally.

Location
The organization will expand its geographic service area from broadly regional to selectively national in scope, targeting those states and population centers which demonstrate sufficient unmet need for services, a favorable regulatory and funding environment and adequate denominational representation to provide spiritual support.

If these positions are thoughtfully constructed and clearly reflective of solid research in each area, I think you can see how powerful they are for boards and leadership teams as they exercise their strategic responsibilities. Any one of these statements could yield hours of generative discussion in a board meeting. Taken together, these position statements need to paint a clear picture of what the chosen future will look like.

These positions should also be descriptive enough to be broken down into annual goals and tactical objectives, complete with measurable indicators of progress. As stated before, however, tactical statements should NOT be under the purview of boards or board committees. They can be reviewed as annual initiatives or objectives, but a board's responsibility is to approve the long-range strategic direction of the organization and not to tell management how to execute the plan.

Taking Action

Once a long-range strategic plan is adopted, it should NEVER be allowed to languish on the CEOs bookshelf. It MUST become a *living document*, subject to review and revision

Question Five

whenever changes in the internal and external environments warrant. I'll expand on this more later, but below I suggest some simple ways to immediately create a dynamic culture around the strategic plan.

The first major step toward ongoing review and accountability is to make the strategic plan the primary agenda content for board meetings. By structuring the board's agenda around the organization and content of the strategic plan, you will be able to:

- devote most of board meeting time to discussing progress toward achieving those position statements
- report on key performance indicators which show progress toward the end goals
- use the position statements for generative discussions, bringing in key staff to provide background information and to report on initiatives aimed at advancing the organization toward your preferred position
- engage the board in discussions related to changes in the operating environment and consideration of strategies to address such changes
- develop and approve criteria for evaluating responsive strategies in the light of overall strategic goals

You might also think about publishing management briefs between board meetings so the meeting doesn't digress into listening to reports. You can list most board decisions or approvals in a consent agenda that would require no discussion (unless someone moved to take an item off the consent agenda and put it on the table). By structuring meetings this way, you embed the strategic plan into governance practice.

Your Preferred Future. Achieved.

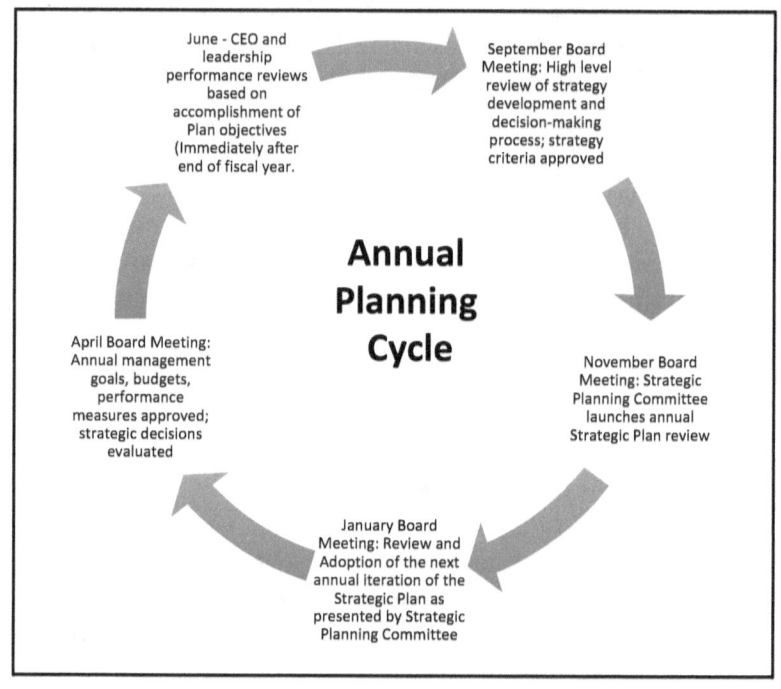

(Fig. 2)

The second biggest step toward ongoing review and accountability is to make the review and updating of the strategic plan an annual event, scheduled for a vote by the board at the same time every year. I recommend having a rolling one-year strategic plan with a three to five- year horizon. Each year, the plan is updated and another year is added to the horizon. If this is done thoroughly, it is possible that a comprehensive strategic planning process taking 6 - 12 months to complete might not be needed again. The following chart (Fig. 2) illustrates an example of an annual planning cycle I developed for a client based on the dates of their four quarterly board meetings (you can adjust this cycle to fit your organization's calendar). The result is a coherent, amendable,

Question Five

five-year rolling plan which is reviewed annually with a new five-year horizon being pushed out each year.

Specific annual initiatives or objectives are developed in this cycle and become the basis for preparing the annual budget. These are specific and measurable action items that direct the work of the staff each year. One client using this approach actually published the annual initiatives and posted them in various places around the company to remind staff of the importance of their work to move the organization forward. They also helped instill commitment to the goals and helped hold each other accountable for their attainment.

Finally, to deal with those unanticipated wild card events, tools need to be developed which allow the organization's board and management to make crisis decisions efficiently in a manner which stays true to the theme and direction of the organization's strategic plan. One of the most effective ways to deal with unexpected challenges or opportunities is to develop a set of screening criteria which reflect the philosophical and positional commitments of the organization in its strategic plan.

I have found that one of the best approaches to strategy development around emerging issues was created by David La Piana.[1] As mentioned earlier, I will share his approach in Chapter Eight and demonstrate how the overall strategic planning process provides the framework for using this type of disciplined approach. I will also provide some examples of screening criteria that can be used. Boards which are equipped with these decision-making tools become more focused and engaged when issues arise that require immediate attention. Tools like this help to reduce stress and uncertainty while promoting clarity and confidence – in the CEO, leadership

Your Preferred Future. Achieved.

team, the board and in your organization's ability to tackle challenges.

Articulating one's preferred future requires thoughtful reflection and analysis. Future possibilities, current realities or conditions that may impact your future – all these must eventually be captured in statements that describe the organization's preferred future and which direct the activities needed to achieve it.

> Know your limits,
> but never stop trying
> to exceed them.

Unknown

Question Six

Can you get there?

This question addresses an often-neglected aspect of thorough strategic planning. Having laid out your organization's preferred future, you now need to determine if you have the capacity to truly achieve that future. Do you have the necessary resources, processes, policies and infrastructure to put your strategic plan into action? Along the way, can you adapt and respond to emerging challenges and opportunities?

A capacity assessment is different than a traditional SWOT analysis, although a SWOT analysis could conceivably be used at this point. In most traditional strategic planning processes, SWOT analysis is conducted at the outset, with the unfortunate result that the desired future position is shaped by an understanding of weaknesses and threats, instead of a thoughtful regard for strengths and opportunities. Furthermore, because every organization has capacity in varying degrees in different areas, pigeon-holing elements of capacity into strengths, weaknesses, opportunities or threats can create false dichotomies and renders absolute judgments without recognizing gradations in strengths or weaknesses.

In the following paragraphs I have highlighted several methods I've used during the assessment process which may be beneficial. Regardless of the method, it is important that every aspect of the organization be considered and that the data from such methods be analyzed in the context of the preferred positions described earlier. In essence, the information obtained must address the organization's ability to achieve its future. And, if there are systems, processes, or other barriers to achieving the desired future, then questions around how those can be overcome or how capacity can be built will necessarily become part of the planning process.

Following are a few of the many approaches to capacity assessment that can be used by nonprofit organizations to evaluate their ability to move toward its preferred strategic positions.

Allison[1] (pp. 158-163) lists "eight areas of operations [that] are most relevant for strategic planning":

1. Human Resources
1. Organizational Structure and Culture
2. Financial Management
3. Resource and Business Development
4. External Communications
5. Information Technology
6. Facilities and Equipment
7. Planning and Evaluation

Thigpen[2] (2007), in her work at the Center for Nonprofit Leadership at Adelphi University, expanded the list and created questionnaires for each of the following:

1. Mission
2. Board Governance
3. Planning
4. Resource Development
5. External Relations
6. Administration/Management
7. Executive leadership
8. Finance
9. Human Resources
10. Program Planning/Evaluation
11. Space and Facilities
12. Technology

Question Six

Individual questionnaires were created for each area along with suggested interviewees to ensure valid and knowledgeable input.

Using most of these same categories, the Marguerite Casey Foundation[3] developed an assessment tool that groups 59 questions into four broad categories of capacity:

1. Leadership Capacity
2. Adaptive Capacity
3. Management Capacity
4. Operational Capacity

Their questionnaire requires participants to select one of four narrative descriptors for each item, thereby ranking capacity in levels 1, 2, 3 or 4.

Levinger and Bloom[4] developed an easy-to-use tool called the Simple Capacity Assessment Tool (SCAT) which engages staff and other stakeholders in rating criteria as "nascent," "emerging," "expanding" or "mature." Their seven areas of assessment are:

1. Governance
2. Management Practices
3. Human Resources
4. Financial Resources
5. Service Delivery
6. External Relations
7. Partnering

An interesting aspect of this tool is that stakeholders are involved in developing additional criteria under each subcategory, thereby customizing the tool to consider the unique aspects of the organization.

Your Preferred Future. Achieved.

One of the most widely used online assessment tools comes from the McKinsey Foundation.[5] The Organizational Capacity Assessment Tool (OCAT) evaluates nine areas using 123 questions. Similar in construction to the Marguerite Casey Foundation questionnaire, four descriptors are provided for each item. The ten areas of analysis in the OCAT are:

1. Aspirations
2. Strategy
3. Leadership, Staff and Volunteers
4. Funding
5. Values
6. Learning and Innovation
7. Marketing and Communication
8. Managing Processes
9. Organization, Infrastructure and Technology
10. Advocacy (optional)

There are several advantages to using the OCAT. Responses are tabulated automatically, and the results are published in the form of a comprehensive report. Not only is capacity measured in a rating scale, but an indication of consensus is provided to indicate the extent to which participants were close or disparate in their responses. Those areas which were high or low in capacity are also color coded. The report provides recommendations for "low hanging fruit" and areas of strength upon which to build. Agendas and templates for planning committee meetings are provided. Graphic images depicting the status of the organization in the various areas are helpful for achieving shared understanding of the overall capacity. Finally, the option for a tenth criterion, advocacy, is provided, but is for use only by nonprofits that have a budget and staff devoted to that function.

Numerous state nonprofit associations[6] have developed capacity assessment tools for member organizations. Some of

Question Six

these tools are free and accessible online. Others are available to members only. It is definitely worthwhile to investigate which resources are available in your state.

Having worked with a number of nonprofit organizations experiencing decline in revenue, members, staff and/or clients, I know that it is difficult to commit resources to building capacity. In the face of downward leaning trend lines, it is very hard to justify adding staff, infrastructure and other systems or assets which are needed to change the direction of the organization. There are times, however, in the life of organizations when you cannot *not* invest in additional assets in order to create the sufficiently disruptive force needed to reverse the downward spiral. This may require seeking a corporate or foundation grant, soliciting a major donor, borrowing from the endowment or some other strategy. When the alternative is eventual demise, however, investment in capacity building becomes necessary.

> Dreams will turn to disillusionment if you don't consider your organization's capacity.

Regardless of how the capacity assessment is conducted, the results need to be carefully reviewed with an eye toward answering the critical question, "Can we get there?". Your dreams for a preferred future will turn into disillusionment and disappointment if you don't attend to your organization's capacity. My preferred future of being able to dunk a basketball, for example, has to take into consideration my aging knees. My brain may say "jump," but my body is just not going to do what I wish it could. If you lack the capacity to execute the tactical action needed to realize the organization's future aspirations, those areas need to be built up before you

Your Preferred Future. Achieved.

can move forward. Conducting a thorough capacity assessment is an important step to being able to realize that future.

The results of a capacity assessment may cause you to rethink some of the positions you aspire to, recognizing the difference between the possible and the plausible. Your analysis may also lead you to determine that even if a particular goal may not be possible now, with attention and dedication to offsetting those current limitations, a goal may be achievable later. Capacity building, therefore, needs to become an integral part of planning and periodic review.

> Business intelligence is not just about turning data into information.
>
> Organizations need that data to impact how their business operates and responds to the changing marketplace.
>
> Gerald Cohen

Question Seven

How will you know if you get there?

You have described your organization's preferred future and broken down your dream into high level strategic position statements. You have determined that you have the capacity to achieve your goals and are ready to develop tactical objectives or initiatives to move your organization into action. But how will you know if you actually get there?

Measuring Performance

Let's say that it's been decided that within five years you will become the "employer of choice" for your industry in your service area. It's been further defined that you will have the lowest employee turnover rate, the highest employee satisfaction scores and the best wage and benefit packages among all your competitors. Before you start drafting tactical plans to accomplish these goals, it's necessary to quantify performance so you can set tangible targets and monitor progress. In this example, two things need to happen. First, you need to identify metrics that are commonly used in your field so you can compare yourself with others. Second, you have to set goals and develop monitoring/reporting systems to track your performance and your progress toward truly achieving your goals. Every time you develop a new tactic or strategy, you need to be able to measure its impact regarding its associated goal or goals.

Here is another example from higher education. It's been decided that you are going to be the highest ranked regional private college in your geographic area. To determine what that would look like, your institution has elected to use the U.S. News and World Report rankings of colleges and universities. These rankings are determined from more than a dozen

Your Preferred Future. Achieved.

different indicators including things like entering Freshman ACT scores, alumni giving, number of students graduating in four years, student/faculty ratios and numerous others. You can craft a strategic goal statement with associated metrics which establishes concrete targets for any or all of those indicators. Initiatives or tactical plans can be measured for their effectiveness by monitoring the impact strategic actions have on the performance indicator. If you are successful at improving these metrics through careful planning and execution of strategies, your institution will rise into the top rankings.

In measuring ongoing performance, I am not simply suggesting a routine measurement of efficiency. In the previous example, it is possible that measures of efficiency (e.g., student/faculty ratios) might run counter to a strategic goal. It may be cost effective to increase student/faculty ratios, but improved quality and higher learning outcomes might be enhanced by lowering it. While there are certainly other factors that contribute, it has been generally accepted that smaller student/faculty ratios improve learning, hence, U.S. News and World Report's years-long use of this metric. This distinction is very important as boards may question certain resource allocations, especially when they are aimed at improving quality indicators that may be difficult to measure. Therefore, setting measurable goals requires the attachment of a value judgment which justifies the importance of attaining the goal. While setting quantified target goals is important, let me also emphasize how essential it is to have business intelligence systems in place to monitor continuous progress and help to project future scenarios. These systems are different than the routine monitoring of key performance indicators like net budget variance and other descriptive statistics like the number of people served, number of employees, etc.

Question Seven

Business intelligence requires another level of observation and analysis. It requires tracking performance over time along with the capacity to project possible statistical scenarios into the future. This may sound complicated, but it isn't. Let's look at one of the statistics I mentioned earlier corresponding to the rate of employee turnover. Looking back over 20 or 30 quarters to get a clear picture of past performance will give you an idea of the ups and downs of the rate. Identifying events or environmental conditions will help you to flag events which directly influenced your organization's performance. The environment scans you completed earlier should give you a sense of the kinds of events that could affect your ability to achieve your goals. Beyond that, the capacity assessment you conducted also offers a sense of the ability you have to influence change.

Being able to look at measurable data and benchmarks offers a reference point that allows you to map possible scenarios that meet or exceed the attached goal. As data is updated each quarter, it's possible to refine the path to success by evaluating those actions, conditions or strategies that have had an impact on performance, and to enhance, alter or cease those actions as needed.

Monitoring the Data

It is also possible to detect conditions or predict possible events that might lead you to fall short of your goal. While not a desired scenario, recognizing the factors that might have brought it about is helpful in developing strategies to avoid coming short of your objectives or failing completely. These possibilities need to be part of an overall risk management system which is a subject that is best addressed in a separate process. Predicting performance based on past performance, understanding current realities and future trends, and tracking

Your Preferred Future. Achieved.

real-time data to identify current trends allows you to be nimble and responsive to changes in your environment.

How you use such data to determine alternative strategies will be the subject of the next chapter. Monitoring performance data must be part of a dynamic process which includes continuous status analysis, using selected criteria to make judgements about what the data is revealing, developing and implementing strategies to ameliorate emerging negative conditions or maximize opportunities that have arrived, and then evaluating the impact of those strategies – these are the hallmarks of a learning organization and are requisites for effective leadership into the preferred future.

Ultimately, if you can't measure performance or quantify the preferred future position, how will you know if you have achieved it? Identifying the metrics you will use to track progress toward achieving that goal is a critical component of a dynamic and useable strategic plan.[1]

"You have to take risks.

We will only understand the miracle of life fully when we allow the unexpected to happen."

Paulo Coelho

Question Eight

How will you deal with the unexpected?

Robert Burns, in his poem *To a Mouse,* said:
"The best laid schemes o' mice an' men / Gang aft a-gley."
Most often this is translated as "The best laid plans of mice and men often go awry." How often hasn't this been true of long-range strategic plans?

To Plan or Not to Plan

Does the possibility of unexpected challenges and opportunities mean that strategic planning is a waste of time? Would it make more sense to address and execute responsive strategies regarding emerging issues? The debate between those who argue for the value of long-range strategic planning and those who suggest that strategy development, execution

---

Strategy manages people, places and things to achieve a desired state of future existence.

But the unexpected is sure to happen.

---

and learning are best, has divided nonprofit business leaders in terms of how they guide their companies into the future.[1] The debate, in my opinion, is unnecessary for reasons that will become clear below.

Let me share two stories, both dealing with the same organization at different points in time. I was engaged with the organization as the chairman of the board during the first event, and as its president and CEO during the second event.

Your Preferred Future. Achieved.

In the early 2000's our board decided to engage outside counsel to guide us through a strategic planning process. The organization had not undertaken this effort previously, and it followed a fairly traditional process involving staff research into strengths, weaknesses, opportunities and threats. We conducted focus groups around the Midwest to ascertain perceptions of mission and quality. We looked at data trends and revenue sources. In response to all this, we came up with the usual assumptions about the economy, market share, employees and other variables. We crafted a strategic plan which projected the organization's current status into a fairly stable future.

But a phone call in the summer of 2004 would change our course significantly. A similar agency on the west coast was in trouble and was looking for help. Specifically, its CEO had left under a cloud, development revenue was considerably down, the debt load was too high and their religious-life programming was neglected and understaffed. From 2004 to 2006, negotiations took place which eventually culminated in an affiliation and merger. The transfer of assets and membership took place in the summer of 2006 and, in what seemed like overnight, the organization whose board I chaired doubled in size. Did we anticipate that opportunity when we did our strategic planning? No. But that unexpected opportunity marked one of the single biggest milestones in the organization's 105-year history.

Unfortunately, we did not have a process in place for evaluating the opportunity from the perspective of the long-range vision and goals of the organization. We didn't weigh the costs of an acquisition against other strategic priorities we had set, evaluate the labor issues or the impact of the merger on non-operating revenue. While it was argued at the time that the decision to merge was an ethical one (i.e., we wouldn't consider

Question Eight

allowing an organization that provided critical living supports to its clients to disappear), we didn't utilize tools for evaluating the ultimate impact. I'm not sure the outcome would have been different, but we certainly would have been better prepared for the longer-term challenges that the merger created.

The second event occurred in 2008. Once the merger was imminent, I was asked to come to work as the merger integration project manager. It became my job to bring the two companies together into a cohesive whole. During this time, I also facilitated a new strategic planning process which would lay out the preferred future for the merged organization. I was already utilizing the approach I have been advocating in steps one through five of this book, and we did everything right as far as articulating a coherent future for our organization. The board ratified the new strategic plan at its February 2008 board meeting – the same meeting at which I was named to be the next CEO.

Then August came and the financial markets started to tank. Within four months we had lost 35% of the value of our endowment. States were already beginning to hold or reduce Medicaid reimbursements (Medicaid supported 85% of our operating budget). Our country was in a full-blown recession. All the assumptions of the strategic plan were voided. The goals and objectives around growth crashed into a heap. We were in survival mode and the new reality we had to face had very little to do with that preferred future we had so eloquently described in our strategic plan. The next six months were spent identifying and implementing survival strategies. Efforts to restructure and find efficiencies were implemented and with sad reluctance we discontinued operations in areas where funding could not meet expenses. Plans to develop our campus and to expand various programs had to be put on hold. We re-evaluated, refocused and hunkered down to weather the financial storm.

> Decision-making in the face of uncertainty requires meta-vision.

I have shared these stories to reinforce the truism that unexpected things can happen that are beyond your control. A strategic plan is a tool to manage people, places and things in order to achieve a desired state of existence at some point in the future. However, the unexpected is sure to happen. Therefore, exploring ways to mitigate the risk to the organization without abandoning the overall strategic vision must be part of the planning process, too. Ultimately, how can decisions be made to deal with a catastrophe (or a windfall opportunity) without rejecting the broad vision described in your preferred future?

There are two ways to approach this question. The first is to have a rigorous process in place for managing and mitigating risk. Identifying all possible sources of risk and developing management plans and accountability structures is essential. In the long run, having a preventative strategy can greatly reduce the possible negative impact of unexpected events and opportunities. It also provides peace of mind for your team and board because they are more prepared for changes or threats.

The second is to develop decision-making criteria for addressing unexpected events WITHIN THE CONTEXT OF THE STRATEGIC PLAN!! If you have followed the first seven steps in this book, you will have a detailed picture of your preferred future. The plan is high-level. It is visionary. It has measurable goals and it is annually reviewable. It also is the

Question Eight

vehicle through which annual initiatives can be developed. But most important, it articulates a set of beliefs and values about the future which can be translated into decision-making criteria. A process like this has been developed by David La Piana[2] and is illustrated in Fig. 1. While his model can be used to craft a long-range strategic plan, the result would be a by-product of on-going strategic thinking and not the primary product. In my practice, I have used the strategic planning process described in this book to create the framework for emergent strategy development. Steps A, B and C in his process roughly correspond to the first seven questions in my approach.

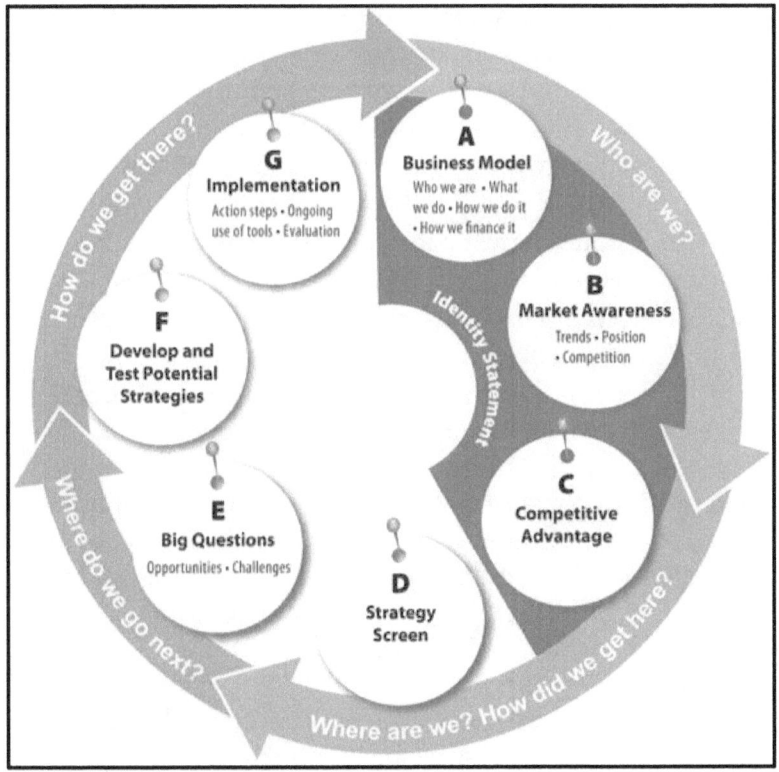

(Fig. 1)

75

Your Preferred Future. Achieved.

Developing four or five criteria or strategy screens (D) affords the organization a rational basis for evaluating events (E) and making judgments about possible responses (F) that are in alignment with overarching strategic goals. Tactical plans and performance metrics are used to measure the impact of the strategy (G). In fact, if you have been thorough and thoughtful in describing your preferred future in four or five position statements, you most likely already have the screening criteria you need to address unanticipated events or opportunities. After all, why would you adopt decision-making criteria that are not in alignment with your overall strategic plan?

Here is an example. Let's say that the organization decides that the following criteria are the most important when it comes to building responsive strategies and are entirely consistent with the strategic positions you aspire to in your preferred future:

- the strategy must support or advance the mission (growth)
- the strategy must contribute to competitive advantage (collaboration)
- the strategy must enhance the bottom line financially (sustainability)
- the strategy must improve the organization's image with respect to quality of service (quality)

Hindsight, of course, is always 20/20, but let's apply these criteria to both of the events I shared earlier. Would we have proceeded with the merger had we employed this screening device? The affiliation certainly allowed us to advance our mission. Giving us a national scale of operations afforded us a competitive advantage over smaller, more regional organizations. We also gained attention from funders and trade associations. And because we built into the merger integration

Question Eight

process commitments to a philosophy of quality service delivery, the merger definitely helped us enhance our image for providing exceptional service. However, the impact on the organization's finances was damaging. The hoped-for expansion of the donor data-base did not materialize and fund-raising could not keep up with a growing loss from operations. Promises to bring wages and benefits into alignment with the parent company only increased the cash-flow problem. I won't say that the criterion related to financial impact would have been a deal-killer, but I do think it may have conditioned our negotiations in a way that would have lessened the negative impact. All-in-all, I believe the merger was good for our organization, but having a screening mechanism in place would have influenced how we structured the contract.

Regarding the Great Recession, protecting the mission in the face of a very challenging financial environment was paramount and we worked tirelessly not to compromise the quality of the services we provided. In fact, we were adamant that no strategy would negatively affect the quality of direct support. Strategies we did employ were aimed at creating efficiencies while making sure that nothing interfered with our mission and quality. Even though we didn't have a realistic strategic plan, out of necessity we developed a set of decision-making guidelines that allowed us to remain true to our mission and to respond to the deepening financial crisis quickly and effectively.

The fear of having to face unanticipated challenges and opportunities while not having rational tools to aid decision-making is the most pressing concern of most CEOs I've worked with. In fact, they tell me often that they can't wait to get through the larger tasks of strategic planning so they can develop screening criteria to deal with events like this. HOWEVER, building the overall strategic framework FIRST

Your Preferred Future. Achieved.

is the necessary prerequisite to creating screening criteria. Making decisions in the face of the unexpected twists and turns of organizational life requires a meta-vision, an overarching direction, a high-level position toward which the organization is moving. The strategic plan is the vehicle for articulating that vision. Strategy screens are the tools for making immediate decisions about unanticipated events within the context of the overall plan.

Back-Casting vs. Adaptive Strategic Planning

I want to pause here to talk about another common mistake that is often made by organizations as they work to define their preferred future. This mistake is usually described in the terms "vision-casting" and "back-casting." Let's assume that you have done everything that's been suggested, and you have a picture of your preferred future. The error comes from taking that vision and "back-casting" it into incremental steps that get you from where you currently are to where you want to be. While that sounds very logical, it is often based on the false assumption that the environmental conditions will remain the same throughout the duration of the plan.

If you apply this thinking to a simple, static, linear design, you begin with the organization's current state (A) and project it into some future condition (E). With these two conditions defined, the strategic plan would consist of the incremental strategies B, C and D. And these strategies would supposedly lead inexorably to E. You can visualize it like this (Fig. 2):

(Fig. 2)

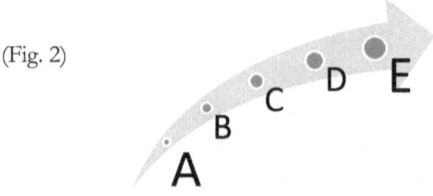

Question Eight

Not only is it faulty thinking to assume that the organization's operating environment won't change, but the process involved in building sequential objectives to achieve the desired result ignores the complexities inherent in a multi-stage approach. It assumes, for example, that strategy B will be sufficiently achieved to justify the development of strategy C, and so on.

The following illustration (Fig. 3) demonstrates the need to be flexible and why intervening strategy development should not be predetermined. While defining a vision of the organization's preferred future is critically important, it also recognizes the dynamic nature of the environment and the flexibility that is required over time.

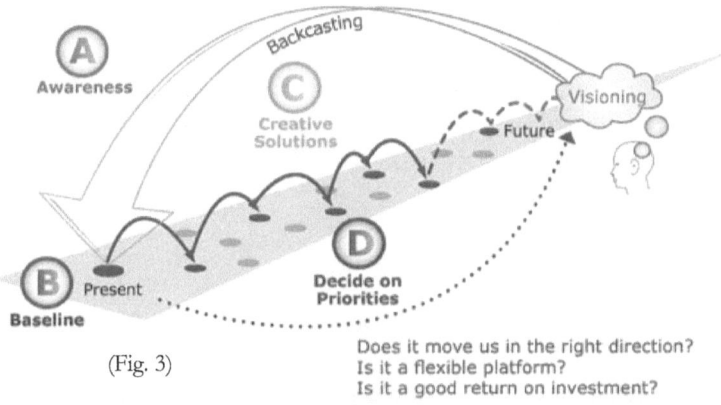

(Fig. 3)

The diagram indicates that as you are monitoring the environment (A), changing conditions may suggest alternative reactive strategies (C) based on screening criteria from which action priorities (D) can be implemented and evaluated. Planning and acting to achieve the vision needs to be dynamic and responsive as time moves on and conditions change. Using a method like La Piana's (Fig. 1) can help the organization remain nimble and responsive by suggesting strategies to address changes without abandoning the overall vision. The major limitation of the approach in Fig. 3 is that when conditions change which prompt alternative strategies and actions, the vision itself may have to be altered to reflect new realities and an understanding of the future, as well as the capacity of the organization to achieve that future.

Here's an example that may further help you visualize these models. Think of the strategic plan as a travel itinerary. You have calculated the ending point, how long it should take, what route you are going to follow and what your destination looks like. Annual iterations of the rolling strategic plan may suggest decisions like taking a different route to save time, deciding to take a detour or stopping for gas or coffee. Strategic decisions which are required to deal with unanticipated events can be thought of as being as minor (making a lane change, deciding to speed up or slow down) or as major (pulling over to fix a flat tire, running out of gas or realizing you've gone 150 miles the wrong direction). You can see the relationship of each level of decision-making to the others – all within the context of the trip itself.

Harnessing the Data

Underlying all of this thinking is the need for constant monitoring and the evaluation of data that measures operating conditions. The ability to develop timely strategic responses to emerging issues assumes a high level of awareness of the conditions that brought about the issue. Continuing with the trip analogy, if the temperature gauge starts to rise or the oil light goes on, smart drivers will pay attention to those indicators and take actions to make sure the engine isn't in danger. Monitoring the indicators of performance in an organization serves the same purpose. The wise nonprofit leader is one who has a pulse on those measures of

Question Eight

performance so that preventative actions can be taken before conditions get to a point where they can't be corrected.

Data latency refers to the timeliness of information and is a challenge to most organizations. In a small local organization in which programs and managers are all working together, awareness of changing conditions can be detected and reported much more quickly. In a larger organization, however, which depends on reports from numerous dispersed operating units, a serious condition might emerge at the beginning of a month and not be reported until the close of the month, depending on the reporting system and the expectations of those managers who oversee that function. Once received by a supervisor, the report might not be evaluated for days or weeks and by the time the situation is understood, six to eight weeks might have elapsed. Obtaining "real-time" data, of course, requires reporting systems that continuously gather data. Investing in such a business intelligence system can be very costly but, in my experience, the expense of trying to salvage a situation after the bomb has gone off can be far more costly.

Relying on subjective and unreliable sources for data may also pose challenges. I have experienced what can happen when programs are in trouble and leaders remain unaware. My organization was nearly asked to exit a state because the wheels were coming off certain programs and our high-level leadership wasn't aware of it at the time. If you are reliant on data that comes from subjective sources, especially if those who are responsible for reporting conditions are also the ones responsible for managing those programs, then you are vulnerable. In this particular case, the regional director refrained from reporting licensing review reports, thinking he could correct problems on his own without reporting deficiencies to the corporate office. As a result of this

Your Preferred Future. Achieved.

experience, we realized the importance of finding independent, objective sources of data upon which we could make judgments about program efficacy, quality and efficiency. This is no easy task.

Having a data gathering, monitoring and evaluation process embedded into your strategic planning cycle that works alongside a risk management and mitigation system can greatly improve your organization's ability to proactively respond to changing conditions. Whether because of opportunities or emerging issues outside your control, you will be more likely to avoid emergency-driven decisions and reactions.

Over time, utilizing such a disciplined approach will result in changes to how you analyze, strategize, learn, make decisions and take action. Being open to new and different ways of doing things will liberate you and your leadership team. You'll have more opportunities to continuously test assumptions, experiment with alternative approaches and challenge each other to find more effective ways to carry out your mission.

> "Experiences, in order to be educative, must lead out into an expanding world of subject matter, a subject matter of facts or information and of ideas.
>
> This condition is satisfied only as the educator views teaching and learning as a continuous process of reconstruction of experience."
>
> John Dewey

Question Nine

How will you support continuous learning, thinking and acting?

If you have followed the approach outlined in this book, you have created a comprehensive, coherent strategic plan that:

1. Describes your preferred future in high level position statements
2. Operationalizes it through measurable goals
3. Includes a set of tools to deal with unanticipated events
4. Enables you to talk convincingly about your strategic narrative (more on this in Chapter Ten)

However, developing strategies to move toward a preferred future is not an end in itself. Implementation, monitoring, execution and being able to develop additional or alternative strategies are critical activities needed to make the strategic plan a living document. How can CEOs ensure that their organization's strategic plan is and remains dynamic while directing the actions of the organization toward its preferred future? In other words, how can you edit your organization's story even as it is unfolding? Following are a few suggestions:

Senior Leadership

The strategic plan has to guide the daily activities of senior leaders. In larger organizations, this could be done by devoting one monthly executive leadership meeting to evaluate progress toward achieving strategic goals. This could contain report-outs by those assigned to specific strategic goals or initiatives and should include metrics of progress. In smaller, less formal organizations, discussions by senior leaders need to focus on the high-level priorities called out in the strategic plan. Even if conversations happen more organically, focusing on these higher-level goals will help keep your organization focused on its mission. The implementation, execution and review of the strategic plan is the highest priority of executive leadership, so it needs to be the dominant topic of conversation. If it isn't, then I would argue that the strategic plan is inadequate for its intended purpose.

Policies and Procedures

Formalizing the various levels of the process into policies and procedures ensures that certain planning and review processes occur at assigned times each year. Included in the strategic planning document there needs to be an articulation of the organization's planning philosophy and a broad annual schedule of planning activities. These should include at minimum the board meetings at which revisions to the strategic plan are presented for approval. The annual review cycle should also include those milestones at which budgets are prepared in alignment with the plan, indication of when performance reviews are conducted relative to achieving the plan's goals, and how the plan will be reviewed and updated.

Board Engagement

Board member support can be achieved by structuring regular board meetings around the major themes of the strategic plan. The majority of time at a board meeting needs to be spent evaluating the progress of the organization toward achieving its strategic goals. Financial reports represent information specific to the strategic plan, complete with scenarios and forecasts. Board briefing materials can be distributed between meetings to share operations reports. Communicating information this way helps to direct the board toward their

Question Nine

primary fiduciary, strategic and generative responsibilities. Boards can help their CEOs remain focused on strategy by demanding more board meeting time on strategic trends and issues. Ultimately, the agenda for board meetings SHOULD BE the strategic plan.

Decision-Making

Clear decision-making processes can be developed and utilized as an execution tool to drive forward the goals articulated in the strategic plan, while allowing for shifts in thinking that naturally exist in dynamic and changing environments. The CEO has to model this kind of continuous strategic decision-making and learning, as well as expect it of the other executive leaders in the organization. The filters and screens for making value judgments about strategic issues can flow directly from the environment scan, business model analysis and capacity assessment that are part of the strategic planning process. If the board is involved in approving such explicit criteria for making strategic judgments, then they are further invested in making sure that plan is successfully executed.

Consultants

First, I would strongly encourage the use of someone outside of the organization to guide and manage this process (I talk more about this in the last chapter). Any strategic planning contract needs to include the development and implementation of decision-making processes to support execution, implementation, learning and adaptation. It may be necessary to utilize additional periodic consulting to advise the board and the CEO on how well its plans are being executed and to offer additional coaching and guidance. No organization should be satisfied with a "one and done" approach from a consultant. The ideal deliverable is an embedded process of strategic thinking, planning and decision-making that extends beyond the publication of a planning document or polished marketing piece.

Business Intelligence

In Chapter Seven I wrote about the importance of data in order to measure progress toward achieving your preferred future. Business intelligence includes any data which informs the leadership team about how well the organization is performing with respect to its strategic goals and objectives. For these to be of any value, however, they must be monitored regularly in order to preemptively detect any changes or developing trends. Having monitoring and reporting systems in place ensures that leaders know if they are on track or not.

Telling Your Story

In order to be truly successful, more than just board engagement and leadership buy-in must exist. The entire organization needs to know where it is headed. The CEO is not just the visionary who sees the future; he or she must also be the story-teller-in-chief. You need to share your strategic narrative through newsletters, video messages to employees and stakeholders, posters, social media and more. Clearly, the story of the organization's future will stay locked in the corner office if it isn't told. Be warned, however, that if you tell the story, and it holds out an expectation, then you become accountable for bringing the story to life! More about this in the next chapter.

Here is how I would summarize the essential elements of strategic learning, thinking and acting:

Question Nine

1. Regular review of the business model
2. Evaluating the environment to support market awareness and competitive advantage
3. Thinking about the values and criteria that are needed to make strategic decisions as issues emerge
4. Developing additional or alternative strategies when data suggests the need for divergence from the plan
5. Implementation and evaluation of strategies
6. Communication and engagement at every stakeholder level

These essential ingredients of active and dynamic strategic thinking, learning and acting don't occur without modeling and the one individual who is most important in this process is the chief executive officer. No other person can inspire and elicit the kind of thinking that will serve the organization in its march into the future.

> Creating an environment in which people are free to experiment, argue, challenge and learn has to come from the top. And this, as in just about every other aspect of organizational effectiveness, comes down to leadership.[1]

"Maybe stories are just data with a soul.

Brene Brown

Question Ten

How will you tell your story, to whom, and for what purpose?

The strategic plan you have just completed tells an ever-evolving story. It provides a setting with historical background, a location, conflict, challenges and energizing opportunities. There is a plot line with plenty of foreshadowing and attention to the unknown. It includes characters who play critical roles and who have the ability to influence outcomes on your organization's timeline. Ultimately, your story can evoke powerful feelings of loyalty and support. Hopefully, those who hear it will be moved emotionally, connect with the characters, identify with the mission and be inspired to share it with others.

If it seems I'm dramatizing an analogy between strategy and story, dive deeper. Appreciate what a narrative creates, and how it influences the way real people relate to your organization.

Be open to trusting that your strategic plan has the potential to evoke satisfaction among those you support, influence an attitude of employee loyalty, inspire respect in the minds of competitors, generate greater engagement from your board of directors and create a mindset of abundance from donors.[1]

You might ask, "How can a strategic plan – with charts, tables, lists, goals and all sorts of other technical information – be told like a story?" The answer is that the form and details depend on the audience. The ability of the story to have an impact depends on the story-teller recognizing audience needs and telling it in ways that are compelling to them.

> **The CEO must become the "story-teller-chief".**

Despite the fact that typical strategic plans can get rather lengthy and cumbersome, the strategic narrative can be shared with employees, donors, volunteers, clients and others in an abbreviated form that meets their needs and brings clarity and consistency to the message.

Following are a few channels through which the narrative of the strategic plan can be shared, along with a few suggestions regarding how to accomplish this.

Board of Directors and Leadership Team

These groups have most helped to shape your strategic narrative and will be directing all the acts. It has to be assumed that individuals in these two leadership areas require the story in its entirety in order to properly execute their roles. Therefore, having the entire working document available for use by the leadership team is necessary in order to guide discussion, frame decisions, evaluate progress and celebrate accomplishments. It needs to be included in board briefings and utilized to generate agenda items for board discussions around the strategic goals and KPIs. In my work with strategic planning, I've included a succinct narrative in the beginning of the planning document that helps crystallize the story for the board members and the leadership team. To avoid having the plan die a silent death, it needs to become the operating manual that drives all activity.

Question Ten

Internal Stakeholders (Employees and Clients)

Print the organization's mission, vision and core value statement in poster-sized format and post them throughout your organization. A little money spent to have this done professionally will communicate to those who see them that you place a tremendous amount of value in these statements as guides for action and descriptors of the corporate ethos. This should also be done digitally if you have screens or other paperless formats or platforms you utilize to share information. However, I would still recommend posting printed copies as it keeps the information present and permanent. The same can be done with the position and goal statements.

In addition to these, one organization I worked with posted each year's initiatives (i.e., their tactical annual action plans) throughout the organization to help employees understand better why certain decisions were made and why actions were taking place. They also communicated accountability for accomplishing those tasks.

External Stakeholders (Donors, Sponsors and Volunteers)

Publish a brief summary that can be printed in a booklet format and can lead people to further information through your website and social media outlets. Marketing and communications staff will want to reframe the content into a readable narrative that is engaging and connects with each segment of the external stakeholder audience. Ultimately the goal is to convert the listener and inspire them to action, whether it be a donation, greater commitment, volunteering or other type of support.

Your Preferred Future. Achieved.

Website and Social Media

The mission, vision and core values need to be prominently shown and integrated throughout the organization's website. The media, marketing and communications staff should work with leadership to post a narrative version of the strategic plan that is readable and attractive. The heart of the strategic plan is comprised of the position and goal statements and these need to be most prominent in any online presentation. However, I would recommend against posting annual initiatives, key performance indicators or other data that might be too technical, confidential or subject to interpretation. How much of the back story and analysis can be included is a judgment call but is best kept to a minimum.

Appropriate elements of the strategic vision can also be shared using social media platforms. Your Facebook and LinkedIn pages can be used to post stories or pictures related to strategic goals. Twitter and Instagram posts can succinctly reinforce the image of an organization moving toward its preferred future. As other social media platforms emerge, the organization's marketing and communications staff will need to discuss how they could be used to most effectively tell the story.

Posting a short video on your website and on social media where the CEO talks about the strategic plan is a dynamic and personal. Focus on motivating the audience to buy into the mission and emphasize ways they personally can support it. I'd suggest spending the money to film the initial video professionally. Additional messaging to follow might be less formal. However, depending on your leadership style, or if you are looking to be more approachable, you may decide to have a more relaxed feel. The important thing is that the mission and strategic plan take the spotlight and engage your audience!

Question Ten

Other Methods

Organizations which are centrally located and hold annual "town hall" meetings – either for staff or clients – can consider devoting one such meeting to the strategic plan and what it means for them. Such high-level presentations are great for soliciting feedback and for better understanding issues that might impede progress.

Organizations which are dispersed could consider holding focus group sessions in remote locations to explain the plan and its implications for the company in its various locations. Ideally, these focus groups should be held before the final plan is rolled out to promote ownership by dispersed stakeholder groups. I used this tactic with success when I facilitated a strategic planning process in the context of a merger. Stakeholders in the acquired company gained access to the CEO and became insiders and participants in the planning process, making sure their regional concerns were heard.

A well-crafted strategic plan sends a powerful message. Stakeholders can see that you have a compelling mission, that you understand your environment, that you are visionary and forward thinking, that your organization has the capacity to change and transition into the future with confidence.

Organizations engage in comprehensive strategic planning in order to identify and achieve their preferred future. The strategic narrative is intended to generate support and commitment to that future. Whether this commitment is demonstrated in the form of money, time, ability, loyalty or respect – the story is told with a deliverable in mind. Telling your story in an authentic way to your stakeholders while

Your Preferred Future. Achieved.

motivated by a sincere passion is the final step in this ten-part approach to strategic planning and is integral to helping the organization achieve its preferred future!

> "Continuous effort,
> not strength or intelligence,
> is the key to unlocking
> our potential."

Winston Churchill

Conclusion

Working through the planning process generally takes about six months of intensive work by the organization. This much time is needed to conduct research and to allow for major themes and ideas to emerge. Although the process can be abbreviated or extended depending on the size and complexity of the organization, these Ten Questions can provide a solid script for success. In very small organizations, the processes may be less formal and may place a heavier emphasis on stakeholder input through interviews. In larger organizations, survey tools, data-gathering and analysis may dominate the efforts. Regardless of size or complexity, this approach to strategic planning is a worthy undertaking.

The following diagram (Fig.1) lays out the essential components you've read about in the preceding pages.

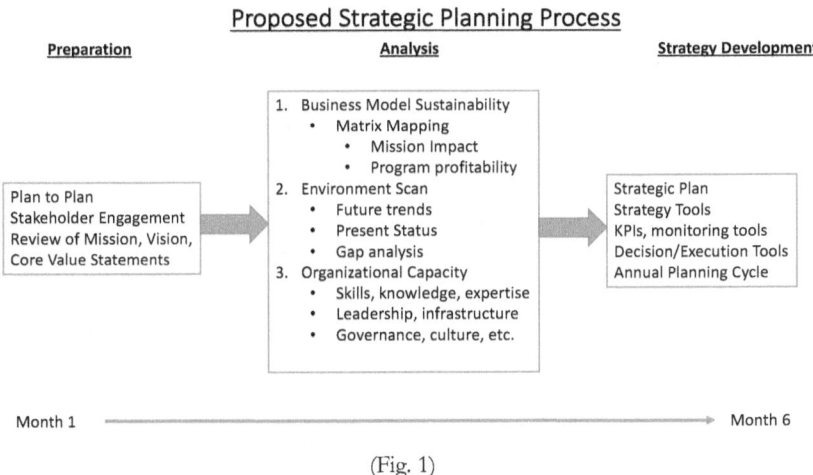

(Fig. 1)

I have found that this diagram has been useful in preliminary presentations to CEOs, boards, strategic planning committees and senior leadership. It is a visually succinct way to describe the major pieces of work they will be doing. If needed, I attach time estimates – both for staff and consultant – and insert dates for periodic meetings of the task force charged with oversight of the project.

Project management skills are very important throughout this process to make sure that assignments are clear, deadlines are met and people who are assigned various tasks are held accountable. I will use a task planning worksheet to keep track of all the moving parts and to review progress at every meeting. Fig. 2 is the first page of a sample task planner which describes each of the steps associated with the strategic planning process. The completed worksheet will include every activity, task, assignment, due date and deliverable from the initial planning meeting to the adoption of the completed strategic plan by the board of directors. If additional follow up steps are needed, such as converting the strategic plan into a set of marketing pieces or launching it through a series of client and employee forums, additional tasks can be added as required. This detailed task management process is also very important to avoid project creep. Otherwise, it is quite easy to allow secondary processes like succession planning, risk management, etc., to intrude into the process.

Use of a chart like this with your strategic planning task force or executive team keeps the focus on essential tasks and promotes efficient and effective project management. For those with skills in the use of project management software, this would also translate well into a Gantt chart.

Another way of describing the overall process is depicted in the diagram in Fig. 3. I use this visual representation with boards and committees to help them understand exactly where they are at every step of the process and to see how the pieces are related to one another. CEOs have told me that this chart provides the greatest clarity for their boards

Conclusion

around why they are working through various activities in the planning process.

However, trying to depict this process in the form of a single diagram is challenging, primarily because it includes both linear

TASK PLANNING WORKSHEET
ABC Services, Inc.
(09.11.17)

	Activity	Assigned	Deliverable	Due	Status
1.0	PREPARATION				
1.1	External stakeholders. Identification of key internal and external stakeholders. These stakeholders will participate in both the mission impact assessments as well as the internal capacity assessments.	TS	List of stakeholders by category including contact information	2-24-17	Done
1.2	Review mission, vision and brand vision statements. Affirm, amend or rewrite.	SPC	Final statements will be established.	3-24-17	Done
2.0	BUSINESS MODEL – MATRIX MAP				
2.1	Define "program." Delineate those missional activities which can be evaluated individually for their impact and profitability on the matrix map, and serve as the lens through which the environment scan and capacity assessments are performed. A "program" can be thought of as a unit of missional work for which decisions can be made relative to its initiation, continuation, expansion, or cessation.	MM, NK	List of programs with brief identifying description.	4-1-17	Done
2.2	Identify fund development programs, that is those activities that directly or indirectly generate revenue to support the mission of the organization and its programs.	CP	List all fund development programs.	4-1-17	Done
2.3	Select criteria for mission impact. Besides the two "mandatory" criteria, two or three additional criteria must be selected to be used in measuring the perceived mission impact of each program. Determine weighting of criteria, if any.	SPC	Criteria defined.	3-27-17	Done
2.4	Develop questions to be used in interviews and surveys to measure mission impact according to the	JB, SPC	Electronic survey	4-20-17	Done

(Fig. 2)

Your Preferred Future. Achieved.

and cyclical processes. The closest I can come to describing the annual cycle used to support a rolling three to five-year plan is the diagram depicted in Fig. 4.

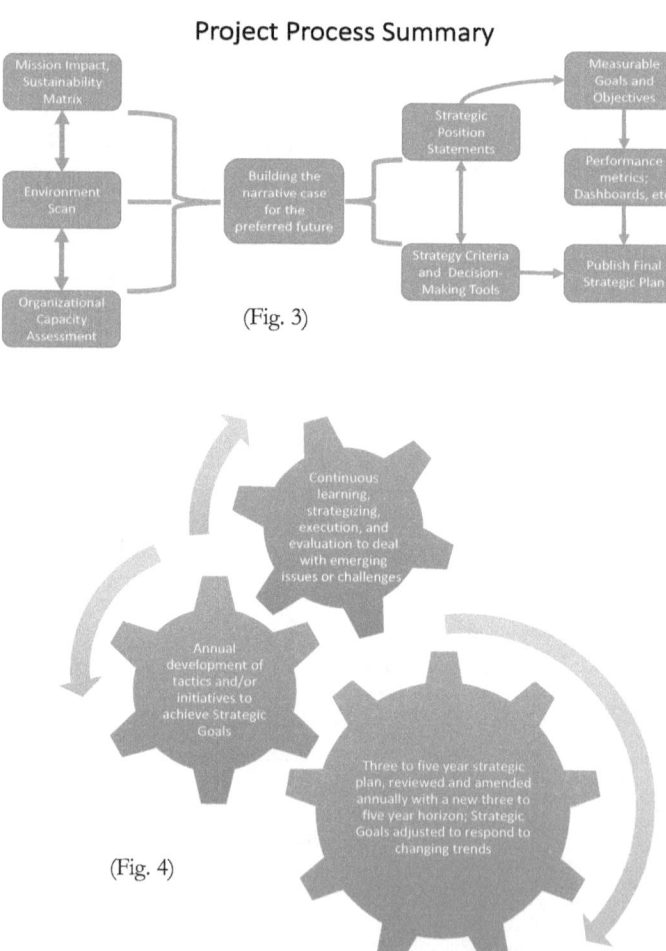

(Fig. 3)

(Fig. 4)

How It All Works
Interrelatedness of 3 to 5-year strategic plan; annual planning update and development of annual objectives and/or initiatives; and real-time strategizing to deal with emerging challenges and opportunities.

> "There is considerable value in being seen as the manager of the expert instead of the process."
>
> John Bauer

A Final Word

If you are honestly and thoroughly able to answer the ten questions I have posed, you can lead your organization through a successful and incredibly powerful strategic planning process. You have been offered the tools to define your organization's preferred future in a way that describes a clear path to impactful and relevant growth of your mission. Your staff will respect you as a leader who works alongside them in bringing the mission to life. Your board will recognize you as a strategic visionary who brings clarity and passion to their work. Your donors and volunteers will be confident and committed to giving you their time, financial support and passion for the services your organization provides.

Considering Outside Guidance

Why should you at least consider using a consultant to facilitate this process? The following are reasons I review with potential clients and may add clarity in helping you see the value in obtaining outside guidance.

Objectivity

Using someone else to facilitate the process allows the CEO to maintain a measure of objectivity and ensures a high degree of integrity. Ultimately, you are the final arbiter of what advances to the board for approval but having someone else to manage the process helps to insulate you from the kinds of bias that can creep into strategic planning. If you are too integrally involved in managing the process, you risk unwittingly imposing your own prejudices into the outcomes as opposed to letting data and research inform the story and direct the outcomes.

Your Preferred Future. Achieved.

Workload
Comprehensive strategic planning is a challenging task. You and your staff will be engaged in extra work no matter who manages the process. But it is much easier for a third party to hold your team members accountable for meeting assignments and deadlines without the additional ties to everyday working relationships within the organization. Your team is accountable to you for enough already without adding an extra set of expectations. If one of your team is failing to meet assignment deadlines, it is better to have a third party make that observation from an objective perspective.

Time Management
You don't have an adequate amount of time to devote to the process. Regardless of the size of your organization, and regardless of your capacity for work, you were hired to provide executive leadership. I know from my years as a CEO what that entails, and you will protect your own health, well-being and effectiveness by delegating the management of this process to someone else. Don't let a process like this compromise your ability to provide the kind of leadership your organization deserves on a day-to-day basis.

Wise Delegation
It is unwise to delegate this process to a subordinate. Unless you are so large that you already have a vice president of strategy, it sends the message that you aren't sensitive to the amount of work or the priorities of your top leadership. If your organization is anything like mine was, every one of my senior administrators was already overworked. To add a project of this magnitude to their plate sends conflicting messages – either, "I can delegate

A Final Word

more work to you, and I don't care." or "I don't think you have enough to do."

Wise Management
Finally, it actually isn't helpful for you to be perceived by your board as being expert in everything. There is considerable value in being seen as the manager of the expert instead of being the manager of the process. It says to the board that strategic planning is so important to the future of the organization that is it worth investing in expertise. Even if you are capable of leading and managing the project yourself, your board won't view the outcome in the same light as if an expert guides the organization to the end.

It is my sincere hope that this method of planning is of value to you and your organization.

You now possess a coherent and comprehensive process that creates a long-range vision and plan for your organization and positions it to achieve its preferred future. It's a process that supports nimble and responsive decision-making. You will arrive at a place which makes sense to stakeholders, inspires support and enhances accountability for results.

We began this journey by asking ten simple, but critical questions. The answers to those questions are the basis of a unique story that belongs only to you and your organization. I wish you every success as you take the vital next steps in achieving your preferred future.

Appendices

APPENDIX A

The following example is from a large, Lutheran, multi-site senior services agency. They described their preferred future in terms of the position, goal and initiative statements I have suggested in this book. You will also note that they consolidated the seven planning factors into five, combining demand and population and dropping "other assets."

POSITION, GOAL AND INITIATIVE STATEMENTS
FY 2017-2018

Trusting God to lead and prosper our efforts, we commit ourselves to the goals and initiatives described below. In attempting to define our preferred future and describe the actions required to lean toward it, we have described in very high and general terms the **Strategic Position** we wish to achieve in each of five key areas. For each position, we have created measurable **Strategic Goals** that will direct our activities over the course of the next five years. And for each goal, we have articulated annual **Strategic Initiatives** that will establish action priorities for each new year. While the position statements are unlikely to undergo much change from year to year, strategic goals may be altered annually to reflect new or changing conditions. It is expected that strategic initiatives will be recast each year to reflect the realities of a new annual planning cycle.

Who We Will Serve

Strategic Position 1.0. We will continue to expand our current service lines through profitable organic growth and acquisition as a way to achieve net positive cash flow, while exploring and implementing innovative, affordable and cost-effective alternative ways to serve additional seniors.

Strategic Goal 1.1. We will expand the provision of affordable housing development in concert with PACE locations.

>**Strategic Initiative 1.1.1.** We will identify acceptable sites for development.
>
>**Strategic Initiative 1.1.2.** We will seek sources and apply for funding through established and non-traditional channels.
>
>**Strategic Initiative 1.1.3.** We will pursue alternatives to self-fund development of affordable housing.

Strategic Goal 1.2. We will continue to grow the communities' business through strategic acquisitions.

>**Strategic Initiative 1.2.1.** We will expand market share in independent living in our two primary locations.
>
>**Strategic Initiative 1.2.2.** We will evaluate the feasibility of expanding into the free-standing assisted living sector.
>
>**Strategic Initiative 1.2.3.** We will expand by a minimum of one new community per year over the plan period.

Strategic Goal 1.3. We will selectively seek development and co-development opportunities in underserved, well-defined, boundaried, "pocket" markets within the metro areas.

Appendices

Strategic Initiative 1.3.1. We will identify and assess underserved areas within our primary markets and create relative priority and development plans for these "pocket markets."

Strategic Initiative 1.3.2. We will develop risk-sharing models and identify potential co-development partners for each market.

Strategic Goal 1.4. We will stabilize and strengthen existing service areas.

Strategic Initiative 1.4.1. Overall financial sustainability of current core operations will be achieved by 2022.

Strategic Initiative 1.4.2 Our brand will be supported by superior quality rankings in all service lines and areas, achieving a minimum of 90% satisfaction, successful licensing surveys, and internal audits.

Strategic Goal 1.5. We will refine our commercial product offerings to create lower entry price points and more product flexibility for residents.

Strategic Initiative 1.5.1. We will unbundle dining services and transportation from the monthly service fees by 2018.

Strategic Initiative 1.5.2. We will redesign service delivery to be more retail oriented, merchandizing services such as food and transportation to improve ancillary income.

Strategic Goal 1.6. We will evaluate new product offerings to attract younger retirees into our system.

Your Preferred Future. Achieved.

Strategic Initiative 1.6.1. We will develop "age-restricted" living options to surround existing campuses.

Strategic Initiative 1.6.2. We will expand core product marketing for dining, fitness, activity and health services to early retirees.

Strategic Goal 1.7. We will create an information services function to assist seniors and their families in finding needed services.

Strategic Initiative 1.7.1. We will launch a "virtual village" by 2018 which will offer information resources to connect seniors and their families with needed services.

Strategic Goal 1.8. We will expand services to seniors in rural and other underserved areas by providing support through the Foundation to other agencies which serve those populations.

Strategic Initiative 1.8.1. The Foundation will develop funding priorities and protocols which focus on supporting agencies that provide services to seniors in underserved areas.

Where We Will Serve

Strategic Position 2.0. We will focus our growth strategy within our primary urban areas, while extending our geographic reach in successively widening circles around those centers.

Strategic Goal 2.1. We will expand operations to strengthen our brand and financial footprint within the metro areas.

Appendices

Strategic Initiative 2.1.1. We will create operational "hubs" within metro communities through acquisition (selective development) to improve market share and create depth of capital and personnel resources.

Strategic Initiative 2.1.2. We will leverage metro resources to gradually expand into surrounding micro-metro and rural markets through development of auxiliary PACE sites.

Who We Will Employ

<u>**Strategic Position 3.0.**</u> We will become the employer of choice in our service area, reflecting the diversity of our community in our hiring.

Strategic Goal 3.1. We will strive to create a highly satisfying employment experience for staff through offering competitive compensation, benefits and a fulfilling employment environment.

Strategic Initiative 3.1.1. We will annually evaluate competitive compensation and benefits structures to ensure that we are the employer of choice.

Strategic Initiative 3.1.2. We will offer growth and mentoring programs for staff to help elevate staff abilities, efficiency and to develop future leaders.

Strategic Initiative 3.1.3. We will offer continuing education reimbursement and encouragement to support staff professional growth.

Strategic Goal 3.2. We will develop alternative models of staff recruitment and engagement.

Your Preferred Future. Achieved.

Strategic Initiative 3.2.1. We will attract immigrant populations into service by partnering with Lutheran Family Services to provide training and employment of recent arrivals to the United States.

Strategic Initiative 3.2.2. We will explore innovations in technology to more proactively engage staff to develop more flexible work experiences/scheduling.

Strategic Initiative 3.2.3. We will use technology to create real-time mutual assessment of staff and managers (star ratings).

Strategic Goal 3.2. We will develop and operationalize an executive succession planning process which is built upon explicit leadership development goals and strategies.

Strategic Initiative 3.2.1. We will develop a "best practices" model for succession planning and leadership development for Board approval in 2017.

Who We Will Compete/Collaborate With

Strategic Position 4.0. We will increase our market share in all service lines by forming strategic partnerships with providers of adjacent services, by acquiring existing competitors, and by developing programs in areas of need not currently served by others.

Strategic Goal 4.1. We will fill gaps in the continuum of care by affiliating with others

Strategic Initiative 4.1.1. We will develop a collaborative relationship and/or possible acquisition of a home health provider.

Appendices

Strategic Initiative 4.1.2. We will deepen relationships with nursing care providers to support a "synthetic continuum" which ensures seamless, integrated care.

Strategic Initiative 4.1.3. We will continue to develop more and deeper relationships through referrals, collaborative activities, and service agreements with acute care and physician-based providers.

Strategic Initiative 4.1.4. We will develop relationships with insurers to serve chronic managed care populations.

Where the Funding Will Come From

Strategic Position 5.0. We will maximize all sources of revenue through disciplined stewardship, focused resource development, and prudent investment, resulting in break-even financial performance (excluding depreciation) by 2022.

Strategic Goal 5.1. We will monitor revenue mix throughout the plan period to assure appropriate balance of revenue sources to mitigate third-party reimbursement risk.

Strategic Initiative 5.1.1. We will pace acquisitions, development and affiliations to assure that a majority of revenues are derived from private payer sources.

Strategic Goal 5.2. We will expand resource development activities to attract new donors to support our services, capital projects and philanthropic efforts.

Strategic Initiative 5.2.1. We will increase the donor list for the ICF by 25% and build donor lists in additional resource development activities when implemented.

Your Preferred Future. Achieved.

Strategic Initiative 5.2.2. We will develop a deferred gifts program for current residents and hire a deferred gift fund raiser to increase expectancies.

Strategic Goal 5.3. Operating overhead will be reduced from 20% to 12% of total expenditures by FY2022.

Strategic Goal 5.4. We will develop an aggressive program of public policy advocacy at local, state, and national levels.

APPENDIX B

This example from the Next Door Foundation in Milwaukee, Wisconsin, illustrates how an organization chose to use a three-year horizon for its strategic plan. It also opted to use "strategy" instead of "goal" and the expression "three-year target" instead of "annual initiative" in order to keep the focus on quantifiable progress and because annual initiatives were less meaningful to the organization due to the amount of time required to effect change. They also consolidate the position statements into five overarching themes.

NEXT DOOR'S PREFERRED FUTURE

In our desire to create our preferred future, we commit ourselves to the strategies and targets described below. Drawing from the seven areas of environmental analysis and building upon our recognized strengths, we have described in very high-level and general terms the **Position** we wish to achieve in each of five key areas. For each position, we have created **Strategies** that will direct our activities over the course of the next three years. Associated with these strategies will be **Three Year Targets** which quantitatively describe the accomplishment of the strategy. These are the tactical activities that management will initiate to achieve their respective strategies. While the position statements are unlikely to undergo much change from year to year, strategies may be altered annually to reflect new or changing conditions. It is expected that strategic goals will be recast each year, and may emerge throughout the year, to reflect the realities of a new annual planning cycle and/or emerging challenges and opportunities.

Your Preferred Future. Achieved.

Recognized as the preeminent leader in early childhood education in Milwaukee

Position 1.0. Next Door will distinguish itself among its peers as the preeminent leader of early childhood education to low income children ages birth to five in the Milwaukee metropolitan area through home-based, center-based, collaborative, and family support services.

> **Strategy 1.1.** We will be recognized in the community for our expertise in early childhood education and as a leader in innovative programming addressing child brain development and childhood trauma by involving our families and employees in a brain protection strategy that includes education on the health benefits of good nutrition, adequate sleep, strong positive relationships, and intense exposure to a language rich environment
>
> > *Three Year Targets:* One hundred percent of our employees will be trained on early childhood brain development and the impact of trauma. No less than 60% of parent/guardians will receive training in brain development and the impact of early childhood trauma.
>
> **Strategy 1.2.** We will demonstrate our preeminence in early childhood education by meeting or exceeding all student assessment goals and benchmarks for school readiness, as well as raising and maintaining assessment goals for teacher effectiveness.
>
> > *Three Year Targets:* No less than 85% of children without IFSP/IEPs will meet developmental benchmarks. CLASS scores will be in the top 10% nationwide.

Appendices

Strategy 1.3. We will support student academic success by providing enhanced and comprehensive opportunities for our families by developing their skills and knowledge through family and community engagement programs.

Three Year Target: No less than 75% of parents/guardians will participate in at least one learning opportunity.

Strategy 1.4. We will adjust the age-mix of students over the next three years to place greater emphasis on serving children birth to age three by intentionally increasing the number of children ages 0 – 3 we serve.

Three Year Target: No less than 50% of children served will be aged 0 – 3.

Strategy 1.5. We will maintain our commitment to four and five-year old kindergarten children through our charter school program by intentionally developing and implementing recruitment and retention strategies.

Three Year Target: No less than 60% of the K5 students will be students whose original enrollment in Next Door programming was at age three or earlier.

Strategy 1.6. We will remodel, reorganize, and update physical facilities as necessary to accommodate a greater emphasis on children ages 0-3.

Three Year Target: Classrooms will receive a score of six or higher on the Space and Furnishings domain of the Infant Toddler Environmental Rating Scale.

Your Preferred Future. Achieved.

Extend **our reach through quality partnerships**

Position 2.0. Next Door will become the dominant early childhood education organization in Milwaukee by providing superior educational services and forming strategic collaboration with partners to meet child and family needs.

Strategy 2.1. We will continue to increase access to high quality infant and toddler care in Milwaukee through our child care partnerships.

Three Year Targets: One hundred percent of partners will achieve and maintain scores of no less than six on the ITERS and ECERS.

One hundred percent of partners will achieve and maintain CLASS scores in the top 50% nationally.

Strategy 2.2. We will become the dominant and most attractive early childhood education provider in metropolitan Milwaukee by marketing our superior academic outcomes, expertise, locational advantages, strong community support, outstanding parent support services, and holistic health and wellness resources.

Three Year Targets: Maintain 100% enrollment with waiting list; Achieve 90% approval ratings from stakeholders, including parents/guardians and partners;

Develop a comprehensive communication strategy which includes traditional and digital media platforms.

Strategy 2.3. We will develop and maintain strategic partnerships that support our work with families.

Appendices

Three Year Target: Development of a formalized system and process to manage and evaluate partner relationships.

Maximize philanthropy to support our quality programming

Position 3.0. Next Door will raise annual community philanthropic revenue to support our "One Next Door" initiative, which ensures the same high-quality early childhood educational experience for each child at Next Door.

Strategy 3.1. We will increase Next Door's community philanthropic revenue by expanding our donor base.

One Year Targets: Solicit no less than 20 additional $10,000+ gifts; Solicit no less than 100 new $1,000+ gifts; Solicit no less than 1,000 new $100+ gifts; Board giving will be 100%; Voting board members will identify five new donor prospects.

Strategy 3.2. We will implement a 50th anniversary community awareness, major gift and capital campaign to launch our "One Next Door" initiative and to fund efforts that increase the consistency and quality of teaching and learning.

Three Year Targets: Raise $5 million for our 50th Anniversary campaign for the One Next Door initiative, 29th St. campus improvements and long-term support for specialty programs. Maintain annual operating support of $3M during the campaign; Increase our endowment to $10M in realized, deferred and expected planned gifts.

Your Preferred Future. Achieved.

Be the employer of choice among early childhood providers

Position 4.0. Next Door will become the employer of choice among all early childhood education providers in Milwaukee by offering a compensation and benefits package that meets or exceeds industry standards, providing personal and professional development opportunities, and strengthening employee loyalty and commitment through meaningful engagement and connectedness.

> **Strategy 4.1.** We will ensure effective teachers in a sufficient number as measured by building a pipeline with partners and parents from which we will recruit qualified teachers, teaching assistants, and other staff.
>
> *Three Year Target:* Maintain an employee vacancy rate of less than 5%.
>
> **Strategy 4.2.** We will offer competitive salary and benefit packages.
>
> *Three Year Targets:* Compensation for all employees will meet or exceed salary survey benchmarks and industry standards. Benefit package for all employees will meet or exceed salary survey benchmarks and industry standards.
>
> **Strategy 4.3.** We will promote employee retention by providing "second-to-none" training and professional development opportunities for employees, supported by clear avenues of personal and professional advancement.
>
> *Three Year Targets:* Voluntary attrition rates are at or below industry standard (currently 35%); 100% of

Appendices

employees have a professional development plan; 100% of senior leadership have a succession plan.

Strategy 4.4. We will optimize the effective use of existing IT programs and applications by providing training and support to Next Door employees in order to improve management efficiency, teacher effectiveness, and to support enhanced learning outcomes in students.

Three Year Target: No less than 100% of employees receive training in applicable IT systems within one month of hire date.

Strategy 4.5. We will build a culture of commitment and camaraderie by creating and supporting social and professional opportunities for engagement and connectedness with others in the organization.

Three Year Targets: No less than 75% of employees report high satisfaction with their work on annual survey. No less than 75% of employees report high levels of connection on annual survey.

Leverage our Assets to support the strategy

Position 5.0. Next Door will leverage its existing assets (including board governance, information technology and physical facilities) to ensure functional and aesthetic facility improvements which support effective teaching, enhance student outcomes, and better engage families and communities in support of its mission.

Strategy 5.1. We will create aesthetically inviting and functionally accessible spaces to promote greater family and staff engagement and socialization, and to ensure a secure environment.

Your Preferred Future. Achieved.

Three Year Targets: All building systems will be maintained and/or upgraded to ensure maximum facility operations. The 29th Street site will have a consistent look across all areas of the building.

Strategy 5.2. Recognizing the expertise of our Board of Directors as a unique organizational asset, we will develop and implement systems and processes for board recruitment, orientation, engagement and evaluation.

Three Year Targets: No less than 75% participation in board and committee meetings. Board satisfaction/engagement scores will be 80% or higher.

Strategy 5.3. Recognizing the vital role that parents play in their child's education, we will encourage parent involvement and develop their leadership skills by strengthening the parent Policy Council and creating and implementing systems and processes for policy council recruitment, orientation, engagement and evaluation.

Three Year Target: No less than 75% participation of elected parent members of the Policy Council.

Strategy 5.4. Recognizing the contributions of our volunteers as a valuable organizational asset, we will develop and implement systems and processes for volunteer recruitment, orientation, and engagement as measured by steady annual increases in kind hours recorded as well as by a X% increase in the number of new volunteers.

Three Year Targets: In-kind hours will meet or exceed budgeted amounts. 75% of volunteers surveyed will report high levels of satisfaction.

End Notes

Introduction

1. As I searched available libraries and online sources for books on nonprofit strategic planning, I was surprised to discover two things. First, there aren't many comprehensive sources that reflect the most current thinking on strategic planning. Michael Allison (2015) is an exception, as is Thomas McLaughlin (2006). They have both influenced my thinking in significant ways. John Bryson's (2004) comprehensive book provides a detailed approach to traditional strategic thinking with a plethora of models and tools. And Peggy Jackson's work on leveraging Sarbanes-Oxley Best Practices into strategic planning (2007) resonates with much of my own experience. I am in debt to their contributions to the field. Their books are included in the list of references and I commend them to you for further reading.

Question One: What are you doing?

1. Pandolfi, F. *How to Create an Effective Non-Profit Mission Statement.* Harvard Business Review. (March 14, 2011)
2. Koenig, Marc. Nonprofit Mission Statements – Good and Bad Examples. Blog at: https://nonprofithub.org/starting-a-nonprofit/nonprofit-mission-statements-good-and-bad-examples/ (2013)
3. Pandolfi, F. How to Create an Effective Non-Profit Mission Statement. Harvard Business Review. (March 14, 2011)
4. Fritz, Joanne. How to Write an Amazing Nonprofit Mission Statement. Article at: https://www.thebalancesmb.com/how-to-write-the-

Your Preferred Future. Achieved.

ultimate-nonprofit-mission-statement-2502262 (January 20, 2017)

Question Two: How are you doing?

1. McLaughlin, T. Nonprofit Strategic Positioning. (2006). John Wiley and Sons, Hoboken, NJ. I especially appreciate Tom's stated aversion to SWOT analysis, having felt for many years an obligation to do it, but sensing that it was an academic exercise and of limited value. Looking at weaknesses and threats as management problems as opposed to strategic initiatives helped keep the planning process at the governance level and contributed to setting boundaries for the board.
2. Zimmerman, S., Bell, J. The Sustainability Mindset. (2015). Jossey-Bass. San Francisco. (p. 79).
3. Ibid., (pp. 50-51).

Question Three: What will your environment look like in the future?

1. By knowledge specialists, I refer to any individual whose academic and professional background is focused on the particular service or product provided by the organization and its programs. These should be found inside the organization if you are hiring the best possible talent. For example, a director of IT should not only have comprehensive knowledge of his field, but should be connected to the current literature, best thinkers, most relevant resources, and belong to the appropriate organizations and trade associations in the field. This should be true of program staff, HR professionals, finance staff, and every other area of the organization. My suggestion is to start inside with current staff and then, through

End Notes

them, to move to the outside for knowledge and expertise.

Question Four: What does your environment look like today?

1. McLaughlin, T. Nonprofit Strategic Positioning. (2006). John Wiley and Sons, Hoboken, NJ. (p. 211)

Question Five: What is your preferred future?

1. La Piana, D. The Nonprofit Strategy Revolution. (2008). Turner Publishing Company, NY, NY. I cite La Piana's work here with the caveat that he is not an advocate of long-range strategic planning. His model supports thinking and acting strategically in real time. I have decided to embed his model into the framework of the strategic plan as part of an ongoing review process which includes adoption of annual iterations and extension of the five-year horizon by another year.

Question Six: Can you get there?

1. Allison, M. and Kaye, J. Strategic Planning for Nonprofit Organizations. (2015). John Wiley and Sons, Hoboken, NJ.
2. Thigpen, A. Organizational Assessment. (2007) Developed for the Center for Nonprofit Leadership at Adelphi University, School of Social Work. The tool is available at: http://nonprofit.adelphi.edu/resources/organizational-assessment/
3. _____ Organizational Capacity Assessment Tool. Developed by the Marguerite Casey Foundation for use by nonprofit organizations, is found at:

http://caseygrants.org/resources/org-capacity-assessment/
4. Levinger, B. and Bloom, E. A Simple Capacity Assessment Tool (SCAT). Developed for the Global Development Research Center, can be found at: https://www.gdrc.org/ngo/bl-scat.htm
5. _____ Organizational Capacity Assessment Tool (OCAT). Developed by the McKinsey Foundation for use as an online tool, complete with analysis and reporting, found at: http://mckinseyonsociety.com/ocat/
6. Self-Assessment Tool for Nonprofit Organizations. Developed by the Oregon Association of Nonprofit Organizations. The tool and its assessment grid are found at: https://nonprofitoregon.org/sites/default/files/uploads/file/NP%20Org%20Self%20Assessment_0.pdf

Question Seven: How will you know if you get there?

1. One of the dangers of quantifying final position statements is that the final goals can become cast in concrete. Ideally, position statements are conceptual and idealistic. They should be broadly aspirational and not necessarily measurable. Goals, on the other hand, should be quantifiable. The caution is that they may become ends in themselves instead of targets to be sought or indicators of a position that may have to get adjusted due to changing conditions. One way to avoid this pitfall, is to annually review the position statements and recalibrate the associated goals and action steps that were intended to get you to that preferred position. This is why I keep emphasizing the need to use the strategic plan *dynamically* as a living document that guides thinking and acting on a continuous basis.

End Notes

Question Eight: How will you deal with the unexpected?

1. The case for such thinking has been argued and was the subject of an article I wrote in 2016: Strategic Plan or Strategy Execution?. In fact, it is a debate which continues – unnecessarily, in my mind. On the one hand, there are those like Allison who continue to facilitate more or less traditional models of strategic planning. The other extreme is characterized by those like La Piana who advocate dynamic strategizing. I have attempted to synchronize these approaches into a comprehensive and dynamic, ongoing process. You can find the article which discusses this at: https://www.johnbauerconsulting.com/strategic-plan-strategy-execution/
2. La Piana, D. The Nonprofit Strategy Revolution. (2008). Turner Publishing Company, NY, NY.

Question Nine: How will you support continuous learning, thinking and acting?

1. Holding CEOs solely accountable for the fulfillment of the strategic plan seems a bit harsh and would seem to ignore the role played by the board, donors, executive staff, clients, families and many other groups and individuals that influence the future of the organization and its ability to achieve its preferred future. While many players are involved in the execution of the plan, I believe it is ultimately the chief executive officer who carries the responsibility for its success or failure. If the board balks, it is the CEO's fault. If the staff rebels, the CEO is to blame. If donors take their money elsewhere, it is because of the CEO. I don't believe this is unreasonable. John Maxwell provided a definition of leadership that I

have found useful for many years: "Leadership is influencing others to achieve mutually agreed-upon goals." The strategic plan should reflect the "mutually agreed-upon goals" that everyone in the organization has committed to. Exercising influence – in whatever shape or form that may assume – is the duty of the chief executive. Failure to either facilitate the development of mutually agreed upon goals or in influencing others to achieve them rests entirely with the one individual who is charged with making those things happen.

Question Ten: How will you tell your story, to whom, and for what purpose?

1. Ultimately, the strategic plan is only a tool to help the organization fulfill its mission and move to achieving its vision. It maps a set of goals and activities that allows it to move toward its aspirational future. One could say, however, that the strategic plan and the story it communicates are only as good as the results they produce. In the crassest of terms, the strategic plan is of no use if it doesn't lead to more money, more people, better services, etc. In short, the focus of the story has to be on results and not on the journey.

References

Allison, M. and Kaye, J. <u>Strategic Planning for Nonprofit Organizations</u>. (2015). John Wiley and Sons, Hoboken, NJ.

Bradford, R.W., Duncan, J.P., Tarcy, B. <u>Simplified Strategic Planning.</u> (2000). Chandler House Press, Worcester, MA.

Bryson, J. <u>Strategic Planning for Public and Nonprofit Organizations.</u> (3rd edition) (2004). Jossey-Bass, A Wiley Imprint. San Francisco, CA.

Dean, L., Lysakowski, L. <u>Nonprofit Strategic Planning.</u> (2015) Charity Channel Press, Nashville, TN.

Fritz, Joanne. *How to Write an Amazing Nonprofit Mission Statement.* (online article at: <u>https://www.thebalance.com/how-to-write-the-ultimate-nonprofit-mission-statement-2502262</u>. (January 20, 2017)

Goodstein, L., Nolan, T. and Pfeiffer, J.W., <u>Applied Strategic Planning.</u> (1993). McGraw-Hill, NY.

Jackson, P.M. <u>Nonprofit Strategic Planning: Leveraging Sarbanes-Oxley Best Practices</u>. (2007). John Wiley & Sons, Hoboken, NJ.

Koenig, Marc. *Nonprofit Mission Statements – Good and Bad Examples.* (online blog at: <u>https://nonprofithub.org/starting-a-nonprofit/nonprofit-mission-statements-good-and-bad-examples/.)</u> (2013)

Your Preferred Future. Achieved.

La Piana, D. <u>The Nonprofit Strategy Revolution</u>. (2008). Turner Publishing Company, NY, NY.

Levinger, B. and Bloom, E. <u>A Simple Capacity Assessment Tool</u> (SCAT). Developed for the Global Development Research Center, can be found at:
<u>https://www.gdrc.org/ngo/bl-scat.htm</u>

McLaughlin, T. *Nonprofit Strategic Positioning*. (2006). John Wiley and Sons, Hoboken, NJ.

Olsen, H.W., Olsen N.D., <u>Strategic Planning Made Easy for Nonprofit Organizations</u>. (2005). M3 Planning, Inc.

    _____ <u>Organizational Capacity Assessment Tool</u>. Developed by the Marguerite Casey Foundation for use by nonprofit organizations, is found at: <u>http://caseygrants.org/resources/org-capacity-assessment/</u>

    _____ <u>Organizational Capacity Assessment Tool</u> (OCAT). Developed by the McKinsey Foundation for use as an online tool, complete with analysis and reporting, found at: <u>http://mckinseyonsociety.com/ocat/</u>.

Pandolfi, F. *How to Create an Effective Non-Profit Mission Statement*. <u>Harvard Business Review</u>. March 14, 2011)

    _____ Self-Assessment Tool for Nonprofit Organizations. Developed by the Oregon Association of Nonprofit Organizations. The tool and its assessment grid are found at:
<u>https://nonprofitoregon.org/sites/default/files/uploads/file/NP%20Org%20Self%20Assessment_0.pdf</u>

References

Thigpen, A. <u>Organizational Assessment</u>. (2007) Developed for the Center for Nonprofit Leadership at Adelphi University, School of Social Work. The tool is available at: http://nonprofit.adelphi.edu/resources/organizational-assessment/

Zimmerman, S., Bell, J. *The Sustainability Mindset*. (2015). Jossey-Bass. San Francisco.

About the Author

John Bauer is the Founder and Senior Strategist of John Bauer Consulting, LLC. He has more than 40 years of experience in the executive leadership of mission-driven, nonprofit organizations. During his career and in his consulting practice he has worked with service organizations in higher education, aging services, veteran's support, early childhood education, churches, civic service organizations and developmental disability services. He has served on and chaired numerous local, regional and national boards including Lutheran Services in America, Watertown Community Hospital, Bethesda Lutheran Communities and Time of Grace Ministries. John holds a PhD. in Higher Education Administration from Marquette University in Milwaukee, Wisconsin. This is John's first book.

He currently lives in Southeast Wisconsin and enjoys exploring the country's rural roads with his wife on his 2003 Harley Davidson Heritage Softail Classic.

If you would like to learn more about John's services, please visit:

www.johnbauerconsulting.com

Cover Art
by
Josep Castells

https://unsplash.com/@paniscusbcn

www.ingramcontent.com/pod-product-compliance
Lightning Source LLC
Chambersburg PA
CBHW021942170526
45157CB00003B/886